Social Media and Your Brain

Social Media and Your Brain

Web-Based Communication Is Changing How We Think and Express Ourselves

C. G. Prado, PhD, FRSC, Editor

An Imprint of ABC-CLIO, LLC
Santa Barbara, California • Denver, Colorado

Library of Congress Cataloging-in-Publication Data

Names: Prado, C. G., editor.
Title: Social media and your brain : Web-based communication is changing
    how we think and express ourselves / C. G. Prado, PhD, FRSC, editor.
Description: Santa Barbara, California : Praeger, [2017] | Includes bibliographical
    references and index.
Identifiers: LCCN 2016031137 (print) | LCCN 2016045498 (ebook) |
    ISBN 9781440854538 (alk. paper) | ISBN 9781440854545 (ebook)
Subjects: LCSH: Internet—Social aspects. | Social media. | Interpersonal
    communication. | Communication—Social aspects. | Thought and thinking.
Classification: LCC HM851 .S644 2017 (print) | LCC HM851 (ebook) |
    DDC 302.23/1—dc23
LC record available at https://lccn.loc.gov/2016031137

ISBN: 978-1-4408-5453-8
EISBN: 978-1-4408-5454-5

21 20 19 18 17   1 2 3 4 5

This book is also available as an eBook.

Praeger
An Imprint of ABC-CLIO, LLC

ABC-CLIO, LLC
130 Cremona Drive, P.O. Box 1911
Santa Barbara, California 93116-1911
www.abc-clio.com

This book is printed on acid-free paper ∞

Manufactured in the United States of America

For Wallace I. Matson and Edward J. Bond
Teachers, Supervisors, Friends

Contents

Chapter Synopses

In "The Role of Habit," C. G. Prado provides a context for the chapters that follow by discussing how the use of social media and the Internet instills habits in users: habits that to one degree or another change them as persons by altering their thinking, attitudes, and ways of expressing their thoughts.

Mark Kingwell in "Bored, Addicted, or Both: How We Use Social Media Now" details that there are many intellectual accounts of the condition of boredom, including a philosophical mini tradition running from Schopenhauer and Kierkegaard through Heidegger to Adorno, and a psychological literature about the "creative" possibilities of boredom. There is, likewise, a recurrent concern within contemporary culture and technology discourse with respect to the perils of boredom. What is missing is a critical assessment of the interface: the facet of a technological relationship that is neither platform nor content, but rather the manner in which the user engages with both. The presuppositions of the subject-interface relationship are the true issue prompted into philosophical significance by the mundane experience of boredom or what I call "neoliberal boredom."

In "Attention, Emotion, and Desire in the Age of Social Media," Khadija Coxon explores answers to the question: What are the particular modes of attention, expression, and attachment that members of the social media generation find most basically meaningful? This chapter discusses some digital technology and social media activities: communicating with emojis, updating statuses, "following," "liking," sharing, and personal branding. It also discusses whether the attachments related to these activities had nondigital precursors that cast doubt on the idea there is such a thing as a social media generation, as well as a less considered attachment peculiar to social media users: a tendency to orient to themselves and others as recursive auto/biographers.

In "Social Media and Self-Control: The Vices and Virtues of Attention," Juan Pablo Bermúdez presents an analysis of the nature of attention, its vices and virtues, and what currently available evidence has to say about the effects of social media on attention and self-control. The pattern that seems to be emerging is that while there is an association between greater use of social media and lower attentional control, we do not know whether it is social media use that makes people more distracted, or whether those who use social media the most do so because they are more easily distracted. Either way, questions arise about whether the virtues of attention will change in the future and whether this will bring with it a transformation in the way we shape our selves.

Chris Beeman in "Does Social Media Interfere with the Capacity to Make Reasoned Arguments?" asks and answers the question: Do social media interfere with the capacity to make rational arguments? Students are writing progressively less well-reasoned essays. The information required to make an argument is there, but the argument itself is not made. Essays have the feel not of being rushed, but that ability for clear argumentation has been lost. Is the predominant locus of knowledge acquisition among young adults—the web—leading to different conceptions of argument making? How might this contribute to a different sort of identity? Might linear argumentation no longer be necessary, except for certain limited tasks?

In "Exclusive Spaces," Alex Leitch defines exclusivity as a form of privacy used to establish value. To be exclusive is to promise hidden secrets: a challenge. Challenges, correctly constructed, offer agency. To be cool, a message or service must be illegible enough to incite an exploration, a sense of legitimate risk, while minimizing the sense of threat. The sense of discovery offered by services like YikYak or Snapchat allows more agency, and thus more loyalty, than other more public services. This chapter amplifies on the point made in the Introduction, "The Role of Habit," and by the Pew Research Center people about how young texters and social media posters learn to doctor their communications with exaggeration, selective omission, and other means to enhance their images.

Paul Fairfield in "Social Media and Communicative Unlearning: Learning to Forget in Communicating" details how digital media and electronic technology are becoming less tools than a way of life, of thinking, appearing, and preferring. The growing preference for electronic over in-person communication ought to worry observers for reasons that bear primarily on what such communication omits, including the realm of nonverbal expression, nuance, and embodiment. As the preference for e-communication increases, what decreases is not only communicative competence, but also the place in human experience for the unconventional, imaginative, intangible, unpredictable, indirect, incalculable, and non-preordained. The forms of social and cognitive unlearning that accompany the digital age demand our attention.

Lawrie McFarlane in "Prices Paid for Social Media Use" explains that since the TV era began, parents have feared their children might be negatively influenced by violent and sexually explicit material, and we are now well past that point. The chapter discusses how the advent of social media has proven devastating, desexualizing young men and robbing young people of basic understanding of human relationships. There is also discussion of the historical role of electronic media and how it enables and invites distortion.

In "Afterword," Bruce MacNaughton illustrates some of the legal consequences of the Internet and social media users' unawareness of the possible legal consequences of what they say in their texts and website postings. The larger point is that most users of social media and the Internet give little or no thought to what they are and may be doing in availing themselves of electronic access to what is, in effect, an undetermined audience.

Introduction

C. G. Prado

People are being subtly and not so subtly changed by use of the Internet and social media. Teens and preteens in particular are having their intellectual and social maturation significantly affected by their use of social media and the Internet. Ironically enough, some of the negative effects of their use of social media are isolating them socially. As worrying is that use of social media and the Internet is jeopardizing their futures to the degree that it is weakening their performance during and after their education. Internet connectivity, use of social media, and texting practices foster abbreviated ways of communicating as well as indifference to evidential support for assertions or claims made. All of this hampers learning and mastering profession writing and communication. The point about indifference to evidential support is a focal point of one the chapters that follow, and the chapter goes further, contending that reasoned argument and presentation have given way to the mere listing of takes on various issues and the drawing of unsubstantiated conclusions. This both supports and is supported by the growing attitude that mere presentation of one's opinions is the whole point of communication and that all one need know about interlocutors is their opinions.

There are undeniably positive aspects to use of both social media and the Internet, and some of these are acknowledged in the chapters here, but the negative aspects are more pressing because they are both skewing users' dispositions regarding their relations with others and, more subtly, altering their ways of thinking and expressing themselves.

Some see the changes that are taking place as inevitable, and as in any case, mainly positive developments brought about by technological advancements. But this view is shortsighted. It is a view prompted by the common idea that the greater ease of contact and enabling of free expression provided by social media and the Internet are unqualified benefits. Unfortunately, the benefits are decidedly qualified. Most central on the negative side is that we are not yet bionic men and women. Our interactions with one another still require nonverbal communicative elements that are learned and mastered, and which work effectively, only in face-to-face interaction where the sheer presence of another or others affects so much of what we think, say, and do. Facial expressions and body language can be learned, employed, and read successfully only through direct contact with others. These communicative problems are being recognized and addressed by parents of teenagers who are seeing their sons and daughters jeopardizing their development and futures by what can only be deemed addiction to online gaming, texting, and excessive participation in social media. Some parents are paying US$25,000 to rehabilitation centers to wean their teens from compulsive use of the Internet and their smartphones.[1]

Though the communicative or interactive aspect raises the biggest questions about social media, texting, and Internet connectivity, there is more that is or should be of concern. Giving everyone a voice on every topic significantly lessens the value of opinions by reducing them to the lowest common denominator. When everyone's opinion is voiced, regardless of knowledge or its lack and perceptiveness or its lack, expressed opinions collectively lose force. Faced with countless expressions of views, too many Internet and social media users revert to simply accepting and endorsing opinions they share. Expressed opinions cease to prompt reflection when too numerous and leveled regarding their authority.

As readers will see, there are many other issues to consider, but whether we approach the matter of social media and Internet use positively or negatively, we need to understand how that use is reshaping people as persons, as thinkers, and as communicators. That is what this collection is all about. The various issues raised, and the different approaches towards them taken in the chapters here, have as their main objective getting readers to think hard about what they and others are doing and what it is doing to them.

As indicated, much of the point of this collection is to exemplify the wide variety of views taken on the Internet and on social media. Contributors vary in background and age, in professional interests and focus regarding the Internet. The primary beneficial result is that readers are exposed to diverse argued and substantiated perspectives, both positive and negative, on Internet connectivity and social media. They are not simply burdened with so many more expressed opinions. But, nearly as important, a beneficial result is that the diversity of perspectives attests to the multifaceted ways the Internet is affecting us—how it is, one might say, encroaching on our lives.

In keeping with the objective of presenting diverse perspectives, rather than presuming to summarize the following chapters from my own point of view, readers will find chapter synopses above—synopses that, aside from a little practical editing, are the contributors' own. I want to caution readers, though, against choosing to read only those chapters the synopses of which they find closest to their own interests. It is crucial to read and appreciate all the chapters to form a clear idea of the many ways the Internet and social media are influencing us. In fact, it is precisely one of the problems with the Internet that it facilitates and invites the pursuing of particular interests to the exclusion of developments and issues of which one should be aware and many of which call for active participation or at least support or censure. This channeling of interests is particularly true of anything having to do with politics. Michelle Goldberg puts the point succinctly and effectively: "Ordinarily, social media users who talk about politics congregate in polarized communities . . . [T]hey expect to revel in a shared sensibility, not to argue."[2] But, in politics, argument is often exactly what is called for. Electronic handholding with those who share one's views is highly unlikely to prove effective against questionable or reprehensible political policies.

As with so many developments, the benefits of Internet connectivity are obvious and overwhelmingly impressive. Most of us have come to value Internet access, social media connections, and smartphone conversational interaction enough to wonder how we managed without them. And, as with so many developments, the potential problems, vulnerabilities, and dangers are both less obvious and their investigation off-putting. But we need to look at both the plusses and minuses. Readers are invited, then, to seriously consider all of the several issues and points of view presented in the chapters that follow. In the first chapter, I attempt to provide readers with a tool to facilitate better understanding of how what is discussed in the succeeding chapters influences each of us, and normally without our being aware of being influenced. That tool is appreciation of the role of habit: how habits are acquired and function in use of social media and the Internet.

Notes

1. Tsukayama, Hayley. "This dark side of the Internet is costing young people their jobs and social lives." *The Washington Post* Business Section, May 20, 2016.

2. Goldberg, Michelle. "The Democratic Party Ruined My Friendship!" *Slate*, April 2016. http://www.slate.com/articles/news_and_politics/politics/2016/04/the_democratic_primary_ruined_my_friendship.html.

CHAPTER ONE

The Role of Habit

C. G. Prado

Like so many social and political projects and endeavors, the Internet in general and social media in particular are having results quite different from what their creators hoped for and expected. Some of these unquestionably are good results. We have all blessed the ability to look something up on a website, to shop online, to be dazzled by NASA's daily pictures of the universe, to "post" our views on issues or events we care about, and to respond to postings we find interesting or requiring comment or correction. But some results are bad, and while most readers will rightly think first of privacy issues in connection with bad results, I believe the more worrying results have to do with how the use of social media and Internet connectivity is having negative sociopsychological effects on users. Still more worrying is the fact that these negative effects are especially impacting young users who are still in the process of defining themselves as persons.

There is no question that the Internet and social media have put many people in touch who otherwise would not have had contact with one another. Much of this contact is through postings on social media websites and other interactive sites that enable the sharing of photographs and videos. There is also more direct one-on-one connectivity among individuals through computer, pad or tablet, and smartphone texting. Just as important as the greatly expanded connectivity among individuals is that social media sites, like Twitter and Facebook, have given people a voice they never had before. Anyone can post a comment or opinion on a host of Internet sites. It is now possible to make your views known to literally millions of people beyond those you deal with face to face. Admittedly, this enhanced connectivity, like all other forms of human interaction, has its own negative aspects. Individuals who benefit from Internet and social media connectivity may also suffer violation of their privacy, defamation, and cyberbullying. Moreover, comments and photos enthusiastically posted by individuals at one point in time may at a later time cause them social embarrassment or jeopardize their career or political opportunities.

On the whole, the Internet and social media have enabled a degree of social interaction undreamt of in the past. It is also unarguable that there are both pluses and minuses to this interaction through social media and the Internet. Sorting out the pluses and minuses is complicated by the diversity of views on the issue. This diversity makes identifying the good and bad results of using social media and the Internet difficult, and a great deal of the felt approval or opprobrium does not depend only on point of view as determined by background, interests, and occupation, as one would expect. Age is also a deciding factor. This is why, in collecting the chapters that follow, I worked to find contributors as different in age as in background, interests, and occupation, always mindful of their perceptiveness and the quality of their contributions.

A collection like this one, reflecting the diversity of views on social media and Internet use, is overdue. Too many available books about the Internet and social media are by single authors with particular points of view and objectives and concerned to make a case for their own judgments and outlooks. What is offered here are a number of treatments of issues raised by the use of social media and the Internet, treatments based on different perspectives and calling attention to diverse aspects of Internet connectivity. The aim is to make readers aware of the more important results of young and old using social media and the Internet. However, it is left to readers to draw their own conclusions.

My own view on the use of social media and the Internet is a cautious one. I believe that while there are genuine benefits, problems are coming up that have to do with users' practices and what those practices lead to. To my mind, the clearest instance of the dubious practices in question is texting, and it is texting that provides the readiest examples of highly problematic consequences. For instance, in a recent article, it was noted that a survey "of more than 400 eighth and 11th graders found that many teenage texters had a lot in common with compulsive gamblers." The point that is being made is that many teenage texters are as obsessive about texting as compulsive gamblers are about wagering. This is an unnerving development. It is a development involving the overwhelming majority of teenagers rather than a relatively small group: "Texting has become the dominant mode of communication for teenagers, according to figures published in 2012 by the Pew Internet and American Life Project."[1] Though the figure is at first startling, apparently "[t]he median number of texts sent by teens is 60 a day."[2] What this level of usage leads to is captured in the ironic title of another article: "Social Media Making Millennials Less Social."[3]

This second article illustrates another worrying outcome of texting as a favored practice, noting that a study "conducted by Flashgap . . . found that 87 percent of millennials admitted to missing out on an ongoing conversation because they were distracted by their phone."[4] Fully 87 out of a 100 teenagers think it is more important to answer a text or call than continue a face-to-face conversation; nor is doing so thought rude, since 87 out of a 100 are prepared to do exactly the same thing. In my experience, giving a cellphone or smartphone message or call priority over an ongoing conversation is as true of most adults as it is of millennials and teenagers. Doing so is usually rationalized as the call or message possibly being immediately important, but the cases where this is actually true seem to be rare. The judgment of possible importance appears to be more a function of interest than of pressing events.

Obsessive texting and giving incoming texts and calls priority over ongoing conversations are only two examples of how electronic connectivity is altering peoples' attitudes and social practices. Some will argue that the alterations are not for the worse; that the problem posed is a matter of properly assimilating them rather than of correcting or reversing them. This may be true to some extent, especially when we consider that there is little chance of stopping or undoing the connectivity that has prompted these controversial practices. But it is very important to be aware of what is happening with social media, the Internet, and smartphone connectivity, and to think seriously about whether what is happening needs to be redressed in some measure.

The chapters here speak for themselves. What I offer in the rest of this chapter is a discussion of how use of social media and the Internet affects users in one pivotal way, which is by instilling habits in them: habits that change their attitudes and conduct, habits that change users as persons, and habits that are acquired and exercised quite unconsciously.

To support my points about the role of habit in what follows, I rely on views expressed by three very different philosophers: Aristotle, John Dewey, and Michel Foucault. Using the insights of an ancient Greek thinker, a systematic pragmatist, and a trendsetting postmodernist is very much in line with my gathering of contributors to this anthology with diverse back-grounds and interests. As I will show, these three philosophers, whose backgrounds, orientations, and central contributions are quite different, nonetheless come together on the nature of habit. That they do come together regarding habit not only strengthens their individual conclusions, but it also reflects the value and importance of converging on a point or issue from different perspectives.

Dewey's account of how habits shape persons was fundamental to his work and writings on education. But Dewey had an optimistic view of edu-cation, and therefore of how persons are shaped. Though he agreed with Dewey—and with Aristotle—about the role of habit, Foucault had a more cynical view of how individuals are shaped as the persons they are. While for Dewey, educative management of human conduct and the instilling of certain habits was a way to make things better, for Foucault, the disciplin-ing of individuals and so the instilling of habits in them only made things different. It might, at some point, be judged that the results are positive, but only because of cotemporaneous interest-determined perceptions. This is stressed in *Discipline and Punish*, where Foucault portrays what histori-ans presented as the enlightened reform of a ruthless penal system as actu-ally being implementation of changes that resulted in greater control of inmates through introduction of intrusive psychological manipulation.

Dewey saw education as the means to a better society and enabling enlightenment for its members. He saw supervised and planned exposure of individuals to experiences that instilled select productive habits in them as resulting in personally and socially fruitful behavior—behavior that made people better men and women through the process of imbuing desirable attitudes resulting from internalization of repeated actions. Dewey saw this as the whole point of education. For his part, what was central to Foucault's cynicism about discipline or education's effects was his concept of "power relations," which cast individuals' actions as always done in a context of oth-ers' actions, and so as influenced by those other actions in unpredictable ways. The consequence Foucault thought inevitable was indeterminability regarding the outcomes of actions because peoples' actions establish con-texts in which others' actions are initiated and affected in unforeseeable ways. This is the point of his profound but disturbing observation that "[p]eople know what they do; they frequently know why they do what they do; but what they don't know is what what they do does."[5]

Despite the attitudinal difference between them, for both Dewey and Foucault persons were constructs formed by habits. Dewey put the point tersely: "habits . . . constitute the self."[6] Foucault's most succinct statement of the point was that "[d]iscipline 'makes' individuals."[7] For both, a person is what a person does. In holding this view, Dewey and Foucault were of a mind with Aristotle, who held that "a state [of character] arises from [the repetition of] similar activities."[8] Habitual behavior makes people who they are, which is why it is crucial to understand what habits we acquire and what each new habit contributes to forming us as persons.

If the claim that habits make us who we are seems too strong, consider one basic and obvious way that habitual behavior determines personality or personhood: by establishing what can be described as responsive continuity. This continuity, or behavioral consistency in taking action given various situations calling for responses, is enabled by habits through provision of a source or ground of largely reflexive reactions to events, choices, queries, and other occasions calling for one to do or say something. The continuity is a similarity of responses or reactions that constitute what others see as an individual's proclivities and, more deeply, as manifesting his or her character. The same continuity is evident when responses are called for in extraordinary circumstances because the individuals responding have little option other than to do what they ordinarily do.

This latter aspect of habitual behavior often leads to significant difficulties when individuals treat new and different situations as they would ordinary and familiar ones. Encouragement to "think outside the box" is precisely aimed at individuals who respond to new and different situations as they would to familiar ones, on the basis of habitual ways of thinking and acting. In a straightforward sense, habitual behavior determines what is normal for individuals to do most of the time, and therefore also what it is likely they will do in unusual or exceptional cases. It is in this way that habits mold persons, and it is in this way that changing habits changes persons.

But how does it all work? We may agree with what Aristotle, Dewey, and Foucault held about the role of habit, but in the particular case of social media and Internet use, how does that use instill habits that shape and reshape persons? The best short answer to this question that I have come across is Nicholas Carr's: "As our window onto the world, and onto ourselves, a popular medium molds what we see and how we see it—and eventually, if we use it enough, it changes who we are, as individuals and as a society."[9]

Regarding the actual mechanics of how acquisition of habits and habitual behavior shape and reshape persons, what needs to be understood is a point Foucault makes succinctly, if somewhat dramatically: management of people's behavior and the instilling of habits, as in education or in what most concerned him, the disciplining of prison inmates "creates subjects out of the bodies it controls."[10] Dewey described the imbuing of habitual behavior less dramatically but in agreement with Foucault as "the formation of attitudes."[11] The common point, though, is that the process of imbuing habitual behavior molds and continues to mold persons.

Take an individual at a given point in his or her life. At that point, she or he is the product of previously acquired habits. Acquisition of a new habit changes the individual to a greater or lesser extent. It does so because the new behavior bears on his or her attitudes, thus altering her or his perception or construal of events, persons, and ideas. These alterations result in behavior that is different to some degree from previous behavior, and the alterations are reinforced or inhibited by how others react to the individual's changed behavior. For example, an individual's changed behavior may prompt comments on it from friends, which may be generally or specifically favorable or unfavorable. However, even if habit-induced alterations are inhibited by others' responses, they are not eradicated in the sense of being reversed and undone. If nothing more, an individual is changed by the very fact of having adopted a new habit, having undergone an attitudinal shift, and then having to consciously work to abandon the new habit and by examining her or his attitudes and practices. But taking it that acquisition of habits does work, as Aristotle, Dewey, and Foucault thought, how does all of this apply more particularly to the use of social media and the Internet?

Examples of how use of the Internet and social media instills habits are plentiful in books and articles warning people about the effects of that use. One interesting example is about not only access to Internet sites and other users, but also the equipment that enables that access. What is good about this example is that it not only calls attention to the communicative and attitudinal effects of using the Internet and social media, it also calls attention to the physiological and related psychological effects.

The New York Times ran an article with the following title: "Your iPhone Is Ruining Your Posture—and Your Mood." In the article, Amy Cuddy, a professor at the Harvard Business School, remarks: "If you're in a public place, look around: How many people are hunching over a phone? Technology is transforming how we hold ourselves, contorting our bodies into what the New Zealand physiotherapist Steve August calls the iHunch. I've also heard people call it text neck, and in my work I sometimes refer to it as iPosture."[12] Cuddy then adds: "When we're sad, we slouch," and goes on to describe how, according to her and her sources, posture does not only reflect our emotional states, but it also causes them.

Cuddy cites a study, published in *Health Psychology*, in which Shwetha Nair and her colleagues had some nondepressed participants sit in an upright position and others in a slouched position. They, then, had the participants answer mock job interview questions, a well-established, stress-inducing procedure. Compared with the upright sitters, the slouchers exhibited significantly lower self-esteem and greater fear or nervousness, even though the interview situation was clearly artificial. Posture even affected the contents of the slouchers' answers to various questions. Analysis of the participants' responses revealed that slouchers were markedly more negative in what they said in responding to questions.[13]

Habits like hunching over one's cellphone or smartphone are not taken as seriously as they should be taken by users. The trouble is that, unsurprisingly, emphasis in published articles on social media and Internet use has focused mainly on privacy issues rather than physical and psychological questions. But excessive and obsessive use of smartphones and pads and their habit-instilling influences raise practical and pressing questions as well as legal and quasi-legal ones. This is evident in articles such as the one published as early as 2012 in *The Atlantic* magazine. That substantial article discussed excessive and obsessive use of smartphones and social media and included the startling contention that "[t]he greater the proportion of online interactions, the lonelier you are."[14]

The point made in the article about loneliness was that increasing reliance on smartphone communication and social media actually isolates people rather than bringing them closer to their friends and acquaintances. It does so because reliance on social media and smartphone communication drastically reduces face-to-face contact between friends and acquaintances. It also does so by encouraging what many misguidedly consider a purely positive result of electronic connectivity: easy contact among people who are at great distances from one another and are highly unlikely to ever meet face to face. There are other, more elusive causes of online interaction's isolating effect. An article in *The New York Review of Books* examined four recent books devoted to consideration of ways in which use of smartphones, social media, and the Internet has become isolating for many and has become so by the acquisition of dubious attitudinal and behavioral habits.[15] A later article on the topic reveals that measures have been taken to rehabilitate individuals obsessed with texting, social media, and the Internet, discussing work done at reStart, an Internet addiction rehabilitation center in Washington State, and a similar center in Virginia.[16] Surprisingly enough, these centers opened as early as the mid- and late 1990s. Though some are ambivalent about its usage, the term "addiction" is employed to describe the condition of these rehabilitation centers' clients regarding their use of smartphones, tablets, and computers for texting, accessing social media sites, and particularly Internet gaming. To indicate how seriously the problem is taken by a significant number of people, some parents are prepared to pay the cost of $25,000.00 for a 45-day stint at one of these centers—an amount not covered by present-day insurance policies.

Some readers might think too much is being made out of what they will consider a relatively few cases of excessive and obsessive use of social media and the Internet, but consider that the foregoing article relates that "59 percent of parents think their teens are addicted to mobile devices. Meanwhile, 50 percent of teenagers feel the same way."[17] A more detached report was issued recently by the Pew Research Center, which provided alarming percentage figures with respect to the forms of daily contact among teenagers and their friends. According to the Pew report, 25 percent of teens—one in four—have daily face-to-face contact with their friends. But fully 55 percent of teens—more than twice the number having face-to-face contact—have daily contact with their friends through texting. Additionally, 23 percent of teens have daily contact with friends on social media sites.[18] This is just 2 percent less than the number having daily face-to-face contact. These figures might be more acceptable if they were about independent forms of contact, but adding greatly to the significance of the percentages is that the friends contacted through texting and social media are ones regularly and readily contacted face to face. That is, they are not "friends," in the Facebook sense, who are at some remove. Apparently, the most common pattern among teens is for conversations conducted face to face to be continued through texting and site postings. In fact, when reading some of this material, my strong impression was that contact through texting, and especially more public social media, is taken by users as corroborating or even validating face-to-face conversations. The comparison that comes to mind is receiving a printed transcription of a verbal agreement.

The foregoing figures make it clear that we are not dealing with a relatively few problematic cases. A very large number of people—young and old—are using social media, including texting, and the Internet in ways and to an extent that are changing social interaction as well as both changing them as persons and changing the nature of their relations to others.

While the habit of hunching over one's cellphone has bad psychological and physical consequences, the more worrying habits that users of the Internet and social media are acquiring are attitudinal. It was also reported in the Pew Research report that 40 percent of teenagers using social media—close to half the users—felt compelled "to post only content that makes them look good to others."[19] Users experienced pressure to embellish the content of their postings and text messages in ways that enhanced their images as texters and posters. Thirty-nine percent of the teenagers interviewed frankly admitted they felt they had to "post content that will be popular and get lots of comments or 'likes.'"[20] What this comes to is deception of others—and to a point deception of oneself—through idealization of one's character and activities in presentation of oneself and one's views. The result is a building of social media and Internet relations with others based on misleading exaggeration and selective omission, if not prevarication. As bad, if not worse, is that the result includes a self-deceiving assimilation of the persona presented to others.

What we can think of as issues about self-presentation go dangerously beyond communicative idealization of oneself and one's activities. Nancy Jo Sales, in her recent *American Girls: Social Media and the Secret Lives of Teenagers*, presents a scary picture of how teenage girls are being influenced and deeply affected by social media regarding their self-images and posting practices.[21] The gist of Sales's concern is that teenage girls are being exposed to pornography through social media and Internet usage and are then emulating much of it for the sake of what they see as enhancing their images and desirability. The core of the problem is that teenage girls are seeing their emulation of what they are exposed to as merely—and advisedly—conforming to social expectations regarding femininity. This leads them to post suggestive and even lewd pictures of themselves and to text and post in a language that Sales describes as "reminiscent of the language of porn, riddled with disparaging words for women and girls." Interestingly enough, Sales adds a point that illustrates much of the above discussion about habitual behavior and repetition. She comments that while she was doing her research, "after a while [she] sort of got used to" the words disparaging women because "[o]n social media, things which once might have been considered outrageous or disturbing come to seem normal very quickly through widespread repetition."[22]

Repetition is central to habit formation, both regarding behavioral habits and interpretive habits. As Sales points out, repeated exposure to "the language of porn" renders the offensive innocuous, and that is in fact and in practice the acquisition of an interpretive habit of indiscriminate acceptance of what is actually debatable social media and Internet content.

A related result of the felt compulsion to post and text content that is popular and reflects well on oneself is that there is a new kind of pressure on users of social media to be up to date and not passé in their interests and in their priorities regarding current events and other topics of discussion. This pressure is evident on websites such as Papermag and Buzzfeed. These sites, while they appear to be devoted to presenting news, do so in

ways that decidedly convey implicit judgments about what is up to date
and what is out of date. Rather less obvious but more worrying is that the
pressure to be au courant bears significantly on language. The language
in which each of the various stories on these and similar sites are couched
reflects a marked favoring of novelty for its own sake. New uses of familiar words, newly coined terms, and misappropriated words and expression are consistently introduced, often at the cost of clarity of meaning.
All in all, the impression conveyed by these sites is that linguistic fashions
now have half-lives measured in weeks, if not actually in days, a development that jeopardizes effective communication by fragmenting our common language into numerous faddish idioms.

What we are seeing is that the unanticipated results of use of social
media and the Internet run sociopsychologically deeper than one might
have imagined or than many are willing to admit. Technology has gone
well beyond the landline telephone and radio to provide the means for
ready communication, means for which distance is not an issue. But what
technology has also done is that rather than simply enhancing communication, it has effectively created what Carr describes as "a popular medium."
Recent technology has not merely improved communication, but it has
generated a new kind of communicative interaction, a kind of interaction
the use of which "changes who we are."[23] As captured in Marshall McLuhan's then presentient idea that "the medium is the message," technology
has produced a communicative medium the communicative aspect of
which has become secondary to its form.[24] It is a medium defined less by
its format than by its content and its users adopt much of its content in
employing it.

What we have, then, is a historically new phenomenon: the use of
social media and the Internet is like learning a new language, and is like
a natural language in that it imbues people with interpretive and attitudinal habits that to a lesser or greater extent reshape them as persons. Think
of what it is like to become fluently bilingual. It is to have your personality change a little when you adopt different modes of speech and gestures.
Using social media and the Internet is like becoming bilingual, but the
effects are greater and run deeper.

To make things worse, the effects of using the Internet and social media
are effects that most users fail to notice or which they trivialize when they
do notice them or those effects are brought up by others. Like most habits,
the habits instilled by use of social media and the Internet are acquired
largely, if not entirely, unconsciously. Internet and social media users are
barely or not at all aware of what is happening to them through the simple
process of repeating certain actions and adopting certain expectation in

availing themselves of the communicative benefits of electronic connectivity. The example referred to above, hunching over a cellphone, illustrates a simple instance of quite unconscious habit acquisition. If and when users do reflect on habits acquired in using social media and the Internet, they commonly see them as an unavoidable part of the cost of availing themselves of greatly more important technical capacities. One indication of this is that concern expressed about and disparagement of habits instilled by use of social media and the Internet are usually dismissed as Luddite grousing about behavior that is necessarily changing because of technological progress.

To Aristotle, Dewey, and Foucault, what Sales says about repetitive presentation of disparaging references to women coming to "seem normal" would be totally unsurprising and in fact taken as quite indisputable.[25] All three insisted on the constitutive role of repetition in the establishing of habits, and so in the shaping and reshaping of persons. This constitutive role, though, is somewhat more complex than first appears.

There are two aspects to the central part repetition plays in habit formation. The first aspect is both presentational and interpretive; the second is behavioral. The former is about what users are exposed to and how they see that content; the latter is about what they then do. With respect to the use of social media and the Internet, the first aspect has to do with what users see and hear on their smartphones, pads, tablets, and computers, and with what they make of what they see and hear. The second aspect has to do with how they respond to texts and messages, how they compose their own texts, messages, and postings, and how the elements of the first aspect condition both their related and general conduct. Seeing the same type of social media and Internet content over and over does several things. One is that, as Sales points out, repetition of terminology to acceptance. Another has to do with emulation of styles: users tend to mimic modes of presentation. A third has to do with establishing currency: repetitive references to issues and topics define what is of interest. All this is evident on the various social media and Internet interactive sites where the similarity of comments and postings, both regarding style and content, is surprising, given the assumed diversity and the number of contributors.

It is important to keep in mind, though, that how users respond to social media and Internet content, what they do about it, extends far beyond specific responses such as supportive or disapproving posts and messages. As stressed earlier, users' consequent behavior has to do with how that behavior influences who they are and become. Repeated exposure to, and construal of social media and Internet content establishes habits, and habits determine interpretive and attitudinal inclinations and practices. As in Sales' example, repeated exposure to disparaging descriptions of women establishes not only a greater degree of acceptance of particular stereotypes and particular terms, it contributes to how users see women beyond their smartphone or pad screens and, if the users are women, how they see themselves. This was precisely Dewey's point in saying that the acquisition of habits is "the formation of attitudes."[26]

Use of social media and the Internet has destructive as well as constructive effects, where "constructive" here is not meant positively but neutrally, referring to the establishment of habits. The point is that Internet and social media use also breaks habits. This negative effect is illustrated in an observation made by Michelle Goldberg. Addressing issues raised by the U.S. primaries in 2016, Goldberg noted that ubiquitous Internet connectivity and social media participation has led to many users being unpleasantly surprised to find that people they considered friends have political views different from their own. In other words, use of social media and the Internet has broken the habit of assuming like-mindedness on the part of friends and acquaintances. Goldberg remarks that "[b]efore social media, we might not have known much about the opinions of friendly acquaintances. Now we're confronted with them every day," because of people's persistence in posting comments and opinions on various topics, and particularly on candidates and political issues during the primaries period.[27]

To recap as briefly as possible, the thrust of Aristotle, Dewey, and Foucault's contentions is that repeated practice instills habits and that habits constitute persons. Again, as Dewey put it, "habits . . . constitute the self."[28] Regrettably, and counter to Dewey's sanguine educational expectations, Foucault was much closer to the truth in holding as unpredictable the results of instilling habits in people. What concerns us here is less predictability than simple awareness. Use of social media and the Internet is instilling habits in people. Some of the instilled habits may be beneficial; others may not be so. We are at a point, though, where what is most pressing is simply understanding that using social media and the Internet is imbuing users with habits and is thereby changing them. Until this fact is acknowledged, there can be no constructive consideration of what is going on. We have to get people to see that they are not merely availing themselves of new technology and that they are not merely taking advantage of new and impressively functional means to communicate with others and to inform themselves. People need to realize and appreciate the implications of how they are engaging with a new medium, a medium that, as Carr points out, "molds what we see and how we see it—and eventually . . . changes who we are."[29]

How habits are imbued and their role in the shaping of persons must be kept in mind as one reads the chapters that follow. Otherwise, it is difficult, if not impossible, to understand how social media and Internet users are being so deeply affected, indeed how they are being changed, by their employment of what seems on the surface to be no more than tools facilitating the gathering of information and contact and interaction with others. The Internet, with its several participatory elements, is a medium that changes us by instilling habits in us as we engage with it. Admittedly, some of the changes may be for the better, but some are clearly for the worse. But the general point of this anthology, its chapters, is that judging whether the changes are good or bad requires realizing that they are taking place and examining just how they are doing what they are doing.

The way for readers of this anthology to proceed, then, is to read the chapters and to think critically about the issues they raise. In doing so, it is important to apply the idea of habit formation, acquisition, and exercise in order to fully appreciate how use of social media and Internet poses the issues raised. Perhaps the hardest part of proceeding in this manner is constructively reflecting on what habits one has oneself acquired in using the Internet and social media. Only when these steps have been conscientiously taken should readers draw their conclusions about the issues raised in the following chapters.

Notes

1. Rabin, Toni Caryn. "Compulsive Texting Takes Toll on Teenagers," *New York Times*, October 12, 2015. www.well.blogs.nytimes.com.

2. Rabin, 2015.

3. Saiidi, Upton. "Social media making millennials less social: Study." CNBC, October 17, 2015. http://www.cnbc.com/2015/10/15/social-media-making-millennials-less-social-study.html.

4. Saiidi, 2015.

5. Dreyfus, Hubert, and Paul Rabinow. *Michel Foucault: Beyond Structuralism and Hermeneutics.* 2nd ed. (Chicago: University of Chicago Press, 1983), 187.

6. Dewey, John. *Human Nature and Conduct: An Introduction to Social Psychology* (New York: The Modern Library, 1930), 25.

7. Foucault, Michel. *Discipline and Punish: The Birth of the Prison.* Translated by Alan Sheridan (New York: Pantheon, 1979), 170.

8. Aristotle. *Nicomachean Ethics.* Translated by Terence Irwin (Indianapolis: Hackett Publications, 1985), 35.

9. Carr, Nicholas. *The Shallows: What the Internet Is Doing to Our Brains* (New York: W. W. Norton, 2011), 3.

10. Foucault, 1979, 167.

11. Dewey, John. "Experience and Education," in *John Dewey: The Later Works, 1925–1953,* ed. Jo Ann Boydston, Vol. 13, 1–62 (Carbondale: Southern Illinois University Press, 1988), 19.

12. Cuddy, Amy. "Your iPhone Is Ruining Your Posture—and Your Mood." *New York Times,* Sunday Review, December 12, 2015.

13. Cuddy, 2015.

14. Marche, Stephen. "Is Facebook Making Us Lonely?" quoting John Cacioppo, Director of the Center for Cognitive and Social Neuroscience, University of Chicago. *The Atlantic* (May 2012): 60–69.

15. Weisberg, Jacob. "We Are Hopelessly Hooked." *New York Review of Books,* February 25, 2016. http://www.nybooks.com/articles/2016/02/25/we-are-hopelessly-hooked/. Review of Sherry Turkle's *Reclaiming Conversation: The Power of Talk in a Digital Age* (Penguin) and *Alone Together: Why We Expect More from Technology and Less from Each Other* (Basic Books), Joseph Reagle's *Reading the Comments: Likers, Haters, and Manipulators at the Bottom of the Web* (MIT Press), and Nir Eyal and Ryan Hoover's *Hooked: How to Build Habit-Forming Products* (Portfolio). Note: These titles are also Internet links.

16. Tsukayama, Hayley. "This dark side of the Internet is costing young people their jobs and social lives." *The Washington Post* Business Section, May 20, 2016.

17. Tsukayama, 2016.

18. Pew Research Center. "Teens, Technology and Friendships." August 6, 2015. www.pewresearch.org.

19. Pew Research Center, 2015.

20. Pew Research Center, 2015.

21. Sales, Nancy Jo. *American Girls: Social Media and the Secret Lives of Teenagers* (New York: Borzoi Books, Alfred Knopf, 2016).

22. Sales, 2016, 4.

23. Carr, 2011, 3.

24. McLuhan, Marshall, Quentin Fiore, and Jerome Agel. *The Medium Is the Message: An Inventory of Effects* (New York: Bantam Books, 1967).

25. Sales, 2016, 4.

26. Dewey, 1988, 19.

27. Goldberg, Michelle. "The Democratic Party Ruined My Friendship!" *Slate,* April 2016. http://www.slate.com/articles/news_and_politics/politics/2016/04/the_democratic_primary_ruined_my_friendship.html.

28. Dewey, 1930, 25.

29. Carr, 2011, 3.

CHAPTER TWO

Bored, Addicted, or Both: How We Use Social Media Now

Mark Kingwell

Swipe Left

What is the interface? Consider the following two parodies of a common activity in the world of social media, particularly among young single people considering dates or relationships using apps such as Tinder, Match, or Ok Cupid. In an ad for the FX Network comedy *Man Seeking Woman*, the main character, played by Josh Greenberg, is seen in various everyday situations: eating on his couch, sitting in his cubicle at work, using a urinal, waiting in line at a food truck. He suddenly senses something is wrong, and then we see him hurtled bodily against the wall, through into the next apartment, or smashing into the truck. The scene then cuts away to a shot of two women, giggling over a smart phone as they somewhat gleefully flick his personal profile aside on the screen. We cut back to the scene at the food truck, where the hapless man's friend shakes his head sorrowfully and says, "Happens to the best of us."

The second example offers darker satire, as befits its source, the still occasionally wicked *Saturday Night Live*. In one of the show's pitch-perfect mock ads, a group of women are using a dating app called Settl. A roster of women discuss the "tons of okay dates" they have been on and realizing that "there's nothing wrong with the men on Settl. They're just normal guys with characteristics I am now willing to overlook." Photos of the men are restricted to passport shots or images of them standing next to the Tower of Pisa, because "that way, we can't focus on their looks." Maybe most tellingly, the spoof ends with a note that, unlike Tinder, Settl has no swipe left function: "Because remember, it's not giving up. It's settling up."

The obvious link between the spoofs is the very idea of the swipe rejection, something seen as all too easy in one instance—the feelings of usually unknown rejection actually being projected upon the fragile human individual—and as blocked in the other, because the illusion of choice suggested by swipe left papers over a wealth of bad matches, handsome jerks, potential abuse, and all too common incivility and disappointment. As so often, the comedy here is a function of recognition: we all know, even if we are not seeking dates ourselves, the ruthless rules of the current mating rituals as mediated by omnipresent smartphones. Not to lean too hard on what is, after all, some rather ephemeral social commentary on a problem as old as humankind's sexual dimorphism, but it seems to me that the function and status of the swipe left is not sufficiently understood.

More recent coverage of dating patterns suggests that a reaction has already set in against online dating, especially app-based ones.[1] But the swipe remains, importantly, an example of how I understand the concept of the interface in what follows. This is a term with various meanings, including ones that extend well beyond the graphic user interface (GUI) associated with contemporary computer and phone technology. I want to use it in a quite narrow and precise sense. The short version of my definition of the interface is that it is fluid space that joins and allows interaction among platform, content, and user. Because it facilitates various kinds of threshold functions, the interface is poorly understood just because, like physical thresholds, its importance is overlooked or taken for granted. What do I mean by that?

Recall the way Walter Benjamin, in the beginning of his well-known short essay on Kafka, uses the work of physicist Arthur Eddington to illustrate the feeling of Kafka's fictional world. "I am standing on the threshold about to enter a room," Eddington had written in his book *The Nature of the Physical World* (1935). "It is a complicated business."[2] Why? Well, for the attentive physicist, the complications of this everyday act, blithely executed by ordinary humans a few dozen times in any given day, concern the implausible physical odds of such semiconscious success. A good deal of the universe's entropic nature has to be precisely organized for one to pass without failure from one room to another. Molecules composed largely of empty space have to stay in good order for the affordances of stable floors and walls to admit use. Our navigation of gravity and restricted space, performed from atop this peculiar upright two-footed stance, must be accurate.

Above all, we face the challenge of mindedness in our movements, the pursuit of goals and stimulus. (Eddington, a staunch believer in a panpsychic universe, did not believe we moved around for no reason at all.) Indeed, this last achievement might be the most remarkable, since psychological studies reliably show that there is clear cognitive deficit experienced as one crosses thresholds. We forget what we were going to fetch, or lose track of the bright idea we came in here to note down.

Kafka's thresholds are, Benjamin suggests, the dark existential corollary to Eddington's physical mysteries. We are forever trying to open closed doors, climb a narrow staircase, or pass from one office to another. The mundane frustrations of physical life become, for Kafka, claustrophobic analogues of our social and mental anxieties, our inability to find peace, and a sense of belonging in a world of doorways, offices, courts, and castles. The restlessness of Kafka's main characters, forever seeking an answer or a judgment beyond the next portal or the next, is at once comical and fearsome. Because those answers and judgments are never available; the doors that open do not lead us to where we wish to go, and the ones that remain closed are guarded by oddball gatekeepers and riddling tricksters. This is the human condition.

We may seem to have come a fair distance from dating apps, but the darkness of the comic visions evident in the two spoofs actually indicates otherwise. Here, we see the threshold function, which is typically experienced and deployed without conscious effort, revealed a violent or, perhaps worse, sending a message of acute despair when blocked. You can swipe but you cannot hide—because it is you, and your desires, which the swipe function at once serves and nullifies. Here, the user believes that he or she is engaging with the content (dating profiles) displayed on a platform (the site, with its ability to gather and display information). He or she also believes that the most important feature of this engagement is the exercise of judgment and choice, in rejecting or (sometimes) pursuing a possible dating contact. In fact, though, the most significant feature of the entire scene is not user, content, or platform but, instead, the repeated finger flicks of the swipe. The essence of the scene is the narrow way in which the user experiences himself or herself through the specific mechanism of this restless "choosing." That mechanism and a user's engagement with it is what I mean by the interface.

Such mechanisms, to use an old turn of phrase, take on a life of their own. Which is to say that, very soon, users begin to experience the scene of one not of judging and choosing profiles so much as one of engaging in the swipe. That is why two (or more) people might enjoy the activity together, oblivious to the pain their happy-go-lucky game might cause to others. There is no actual pain, because the profiles are not, in any real sense, actual people. The profiles exist, we might say, entirely to serve the interests of the mechanism of swiping. This is not the stated goal of such sites, to state the obvious, nor is it the reason most people enter into such engagements. My suggestion is that the interface has an effect on presumed subjectivity—the supposed site of judging and choosing—such that the subjectivity of the user is altered in ways that may not be evident to the user himself or herself, especially not right away.

There is an analogue to addiction here, but it is only partial. An addict derives short-term pleasure from the satisfaction of his first-order desires. In many cases, this first-order desire is at odds with a second-order desire not to fall prey, once again, to the allure of the drug or stimulus. But there are also cases of willing addiction and, more significantly, a strong element of temporality in the experience of addiction. This temporal dimension is far more complex than the usual short-term/long-term framework of crude addiction analysis. Desire for a given drug may wax and wane, and also be rationalized and resented in countless shades of nuance, before there is a definitive use of the drug or a confirmed judgment (whatever that might mean, exactly) that someone is an addict.

Neil Levy, for example, has argued persuasively that addiction is not incompatible with fairly robust conceptions of autonomy. "So why do addicts consume their drugs? The short and only somewhat misleading answer is that they take drugs because they want to," he writes. "The addict is not carried away by her desires in the way in which, in Aristotle's illustration of nonvoluntariness, a man is carried across the road by the wind. The point is not that there is no such thing as compulsion by forces internal to the agent. The point is that, whether or not there are compulsive psychological forces, addictive desires are not among them."[3]

Levy does not deny that addiction is often unwanted and harmful, or indeed that it is an impairment to full, flourishing autonomy. Rather, he argues that we should understand addiction as "characterized by an oscillation in the preferences of the addict. Most of the time, the addict sincerely disavows her addiction and wishes to be rid of it. But she regularly changes her mind; when she does, she genuinely prefers consumption to abstention."[4] This temporal aspect of addiction is too often neglected, as if the condition were a steady-state compromise of healthy desires by unhealthy ones. No, the addict is much more likely to experience deficits of healthy desire over time, impairing a global sense of self—what Levy calls "extended agency." This argument highlights less the failures of the addict to extend her will across time, though that is a valid description of addiction, and more the rarity of achieving globally healthy selfhood in the first place.

The interface is not necessarily addictive even in this autonomy-compatible sense, since it really functions as a deferral of desire satisfaction combined with a substitution of its mechanism for the original desires that brought someone to the scene. This becomes evident when we compare other examples of the interface, such as the search library function available within music storage sites or computer software. Here, we can observe the very same restlessness and failures of choice associated with the dating apps. I scroll and scroll for something to listen to, but never settle on anything; soon, the act of scrolling itself is the activity I am engaged in, which is offering me pleasure. A similar example is the constant scroll feature of online news sources, blogs, and (notoriously) Facebook. One can never come to the end of such experiences: there is always more being added to the feed—suggestive word—and hence no opportunity for even the momentary sense of satisfaction experienced by the addict or, a fortiori, someone with a less troubled relation to their own desires.

The person caught up in the interface is, in this sense, worse off even than the addict, at least those of the unwilling variant. The analogy to the willing addict is closest—though it is worth bearing in mind that the willing addict looks a lot like a "healthy" person, except for the adverse effects of the drug or stimulus. As the heroin-addicted narrator of Irvine Welsh's novel *Trainspotting* (1993; film adaptation 1996) puts it, critics may be right to point out the harms of drugs but "what they forget is the pleasure of it. Otherwise we wouldn't do it. After all, we're not fucking stupid."

What seems most prominent about the everyday experiences of the interface is that, despite the giggling over phones, they are not satisfying, even momentarily or at the expense of future well-being. The continuous nature of the scrolling or swiping seems to negate the very possibility of a satisfied desire. Instead, what we see here is desire out of gear—not in the sense of an impasse or stall, such as one might experience in procrastination, but rather in the way that an engine stuck in neutral can redline its revolutions without producing any traction whatsoever. Once more, the analogy is not entirely perfect: the swipe and scroll offer a repetitive action that can have an almost mesmerizing effect on the user wrapped in the low-level rapture of desire without object; but it is not obvious just what harms this experience brings to the user, except perhaps in the obvious sense that she or he is devoting time to it that might be better deployed, even in her or his own terms, on something else.

The relatively pleasant aspect of these engagements often masks a deeper issue. I do not just mean the irony that the original desires—for a date, for some music to listen to, for an article or post to read online—are obliterated. It is also the case the underlying restlessness of the interface experience hides problems with the world and meaning that are familiar to philosophical and psychological students of boredom. And so, I turn next to that most un-boring of topics.

Restless

Boredom is one of the most common of human experiences, yet it seems continually to defy complete understanding. We all know what it is to feel bored, but what exactly prompts, constitutes, or follows from the condition of boredom is far less obvious. Is boredom a function of leisure, such that there was, as some critics have argued, no such thing as boredom before, say, the age of Schopenhauer? Or is medieval accidie perhaps the appropriate forebear, tinged with sinfulness as well as the routine despair of not wanting to do anything in particular? Does boredom tangle desire or personal conditions or both? That is, when I stare at the full refrigerator and complain that there is nothing to eat, or when I scan a hundred cable channels and find nothing to watch, who or what exactly is to blame?

No surprise then that there are many intellectual accounts of the condition of boredom, or its cognates. This includes both a distinguished philosophical mini tradition running from (at least) Schopenhauer and Kierkegaard through Heidegger to Adorno, and a lively recent psychological literature about the "creative" possibilities of boredom. There is, likewise, a recurrent concern within contemporary discourse about technology and culture about the perils of boredom, how it can be identified and addressed by various instruments, and why this is presumptively necessary.

What is missing is a critical assessment of the complex relation, itself ideological, among these various discourses. The present investigation seeks to provide this, or at least a beginning to it. A significant feature of my proposed structural analysis is that it addresses the very notion of the interface as something with which the "ordinary" subject is presumed to interact, but which is itself rendered almost invisible. We shall find that the presuppositions of the subject-interface relationship are the true issue prompted into philosophical significance by the mundane experience of boredom.

To cash out these claims requires all of the following: (a) a fairly detailed assessment of the traditional philosophical discourse about boredom; (b) a critical analysis of what I will call the "domesticating" tendencies of much boredom discourse; and most importantly (c) a renewed insistence on the background structural conditions, especially the conditions of cultural production and consumption that mark what we should begin to call neoliberal boredom. These last conditions embrace insights, already mentioned, concerning the quasi-addictive behavior of media users, especially as recently analyzed by Michael Schulson; they also include practical issues of blaming or reforming users, and the potential regulation of the interface.

In short, the structure of the interface has now supplanted the role once played by content itself, such that our primary posture of consumption is no longer with the target material—whose delay or absence once promoted the experience of boredom—but with the mechanism of delivery. Boredom now consists not so much in "the paradoxical wish for a desire," as the psychoanalyst Adam Phillips put it, but in the ever-renewable condition of no longer seeking a specific desire at all. The content has been superseded by the platform, and our immersion in the platform is, according to critic Nicholas Carr, a new form of consumption. "In a world dense with stuff," Carr writes, "a captivating interface is the perfect consumer good. It packages the very act of consumption as a product. We consume our consuming." True enough; but so stated, this claim in itself does not go far enough. The perfect consumer good is not just the interface, or even our consumption of consumption within it, but rather the self-devouring action of the immersion itself. This is the perfect consumption of oneself as perfect consumer.

The larger implications of this later claim are just now beginning to reveal themselves, in particular those relating to selfhood and subjectivity. In our time, the fusion of technology, specifically media, with human subjects—more accurately, the subject positions of what Gilles Deleuze called dividuals, multiply divided selves—is a fact so central that, as in the parable of the fish who cannot know water, we are in danger of occluding the conditions of our being. Relations with the interface, carried out on multiple platforms, actually become the sum total of the self's relation to its own conditions of possibility—but these conditions are thereby rendered invisible. Boredom is here best understood less as a disagreeable condition to be obliterated and more as a symptom whose mild discomfort signals a deeper malaise. We find not only that we cannot easily live apart from the interface, but also that the promises of the interface—the content allegedly to be delivered by the platform—is a sly seduction. The interface looms not just larger than content, but also larger than ourselves as we (so we believe) seek the content.

In all previous models of boredom, whether the ultimate conclusion was positive (Heidegger's boredom as existential "attunement", say, or the psychological claims for creative boredom) or negative (Adorno's account of boredom as capitalist enslavement, New Urbanist warnings against boring streetscapes), the self in question is presumed stable and available to experience. That is, whether we seek boredom, fear it, domesticate it, or revile it, the philosophical status of the implied subjects of boredom is mostly opaque because it is presupposed to be already understood.

Even in these accounts, perhaps especially in Heidegger and the psychoanalytic literature, there is a sense that this will not entirely do: boredom is not so much a feature of the given landscape as of the figure confronting, or simply finding itself within, the landscape. With a new sense of the stakes, revealed by analysis of the interface-dominant features of neoliberal boredom, I propose that we may gain even greater insight about the various destabilized and spectral qualities of the "self" prone to prolonged sojourns with the interface.

What does boredom reveal about fractured or spectral subjectivity? We can begin to flesh out an answer by categorizing more precisely the different accounts of the condition. Or I should say "conditions," because one obvious initial insight here is that the experience in play may be quite different depending on the theoretical framework used to critique or (less often) celebrate it. As always, we must be aware that conceptual schemes, especially methodological ones, exist in order to produce the sort of results they are themselves fashioned to pick out.

1. Boredom as philosophically originary: The standard philosophical accounts of boredom bear a common air of mild self-congratulation under their various differences of emphasis. Schopenhauer, Kierkegaard, and Heidegger are the prominent figures here, each suggesting that the subjectively unpleasant experience of boredom is philosophically revelatory. Put crudely, the notion is that the experience of finding oneself bored induces an existential crisis of dimensions serious enough to throw one's easygoing selfhood into question. Why are my desires so tangled that I cannot frame a single coherent one, instead lurching from impasse to impasse? It has been said with some justice that boredom is a condition that only emerges with modernity, with its opportunities for aimless desire and time without explicit purpose. We could go farther: boredom may be the essential feature of the modern

condition, since it marks the state of the self as confused concerning its own routes to satisfaction.

I will not pursue this exegesis of philosophical boredom further here, having written at length about it elsewhere; but it is worth emphasizing that not only does this conception of boredom mark the condition as philosophically originary, but also that this philosophical conception is the originary account of boredom. That is, these philosophers' understanding of boredom as a crisis of selfhood and desire that must be embraced is what we ought to regard as the standard view of boredom, against which other (especially more contemporary) notions are advanced. This is significant for present purposes because a return to philosophical boredom—as distinct from the notions of boredom that seek to nullify it, or deflect it—is part of the critical argument I am advancing. I will also add a political dimension to this return, based in part on Adorno's account of boredom (see 2), but with contemporary twists.

2. "Creative" boredom: The emergent psychological literature is arguably not only a more scientific, but also more domesticated, version of the sorts of claims made in (1). That is, here boredom is understood as once more subjectively unpleasant but possibly productive. The natural adjunct to this literature is the rival psychological literature on the cognitive and even physical harms of boredom. Both of these rival, sometimes indeed impasse, discourses tend to dominate in everyday discourse about boredom, especially with respect to technology, the built environment, and workplaces.

    Consider, for example, one recent defense of boredom as ultimately enlivening argued that a little boredom goes a long way to making the world at large more interesting. "Boredom is understood as that frustrating experience of wanting but being unable to engage in satisfying activity," writer Rosecrans Baldwin opined. "But it's an extremely short-lived emotion, and perfect for airports, sidewalks, afternoons in the woods. Maybe two minutes pass before I've found something worthy of note." Furthermore, "Something I've figured out in my boredom: To be at all smart, I need time to be stupid. Silent time—marked by barking dogs and traffic screeches and the murmurings of neighbors watching old movies. Time that's reserved to be listless and absent-minded not only reinvigorates my desire in being interested in things, it gives me the energy to be interesting, or at least try."

    Baldwin went on the cite how his routine experiences of boredom—waiting in a line for bureaucratic service, for example—highlighted the pleasure he took in overhearing another person having a minor meltdown in the same setting.[5] Most vividly, his everyday boredom leads him into an encounter with a crackhead screenwriter. Whether this counts as "creative" is, of course, open to debate.

    The psychological literature has been more precise in its findings, but not much more illuminating about what counts as creative. "Boredom is, paradoxically, a motivating force/catalyst for action," a 2014 study argues. "Boredom might stimulate the need to redecorate, take up a new hobby, or look for a new job. The feeling, then, can induce challenge-seeking behavior, and therein lies the paradox that boredom, associated by many with lethargy, can actually be energizing, inspiring a search for 'change and variety.'"[6]

But when we examine the psychological literature, we really see a therapeutic program to redeem boredom. By repositioning its presumptively negative features as opportunities for creative thought, boredom is effectively redefined (and defanged) as daydreaming, woolgathering, brainstorming, and other "outside the box" or "lateral thinking" tactics. This tactical taming or domestication of boredom is actually the opposite of philosophical boredom, which promises not future relief, but renewed anxiety. The alleged creative boredom can only take boredom half-seriously.

3.   Political boredom: Adorno's account of the dangers of "leisure" or "free time" under capitalism is the core text here. There is, notably, overlap with some of the negative claims in (2), especially about the conceptual pairing of work and leisure, which Adorno implicates as a standard capitalist enveloping move: the time free from work is not genuine leisure at all, in the Aristotelian sense, merely a sly continuance of the work regime's total domination of the self. This analysis is not only valid, but also badly in need of updating with respect to all of work, time, capital, and technology.

Thus, there is not nearly enough emphasis in the current discourses devoted to boredom and technology on the specifically political dimensions of the subject. Even in those cases where Adorno's account is considered—for example, television and leisure time—there is little attempt to update critical considerations for the peculiar and unprecedented conditions of our world, which is in fact the non-world of the interface. People do not watch television in the way they used to, after all, nor is leisure time confined to evenings and weekends understood as distinct from (and so an unwitting enabler of) work-time. Any critique of the current state of subjectivity and its relations to media must take full account of the urgency of the issue, not with further hand-wringing or laying of blame, but with nuanced structural analysis. Boredom is not simply a mildly irritating everyday experience, nor is it an existential condition beyond further investigation; it is, in its own peculiar way, a call to arms.

4.   Psychoanalytic boredom: As in Kierkegaard, the closest cousin in the traditional philosophical discourse on boredom, the focus here is on what we might call "tangles of desire"—when desires conflict or do not align between first and second orders, when specific desire is numbingly absent, and so on. All accounts of boredom, the ones centered on analysis of desire, especially desire tangled, come closest to the true stakes of this everyday experience. Too often lacking, however, is the social and structural dimensions of the tangles, especially in relation to capital and technological conditions of the day.

Adam Phillips begins one of his best essays this way: "Every adult remembers, among many other things, the great ennui of childhood, and every child's life is punctuated by spells of boredom: that state of suspended anticipation in which things are started and nothing begins, the mood of diffuse restlessness which contains that most absurd and paradoxical wish, the wish for a desire."[7] The wish for a desire highlights a genuine paradox, unlike the merely instrumental one of creative boredom. The stall of desire acting against itself is the beginning, not the end, of boredom. And thus, boredom must always be understood in terms of desire. If we are to explore the mystery of consciousness rather than cover it over with tactics of deflection and obfuscation, we cannot proceed otherwise. The currently dominant conception of boredom, however, performs precisely this kind of deflection and obfuscation.

5. Neoliberal boredom: The pressing need for critical analysis of neoliberal boredom is rooted partly in perceived deficiencies of other literatures, but more seriously in the unremarked challenges to presumed stable subjectivity that are alive in this evolving experience. Neoliberal boredom means not just the peculiar boredom of the interface consumed in place of the content, but the distinct experience of subjective emplacement associated with that consumption—what turns out to be, indeed, self-consumption.

All these accounts of boredom share this conviction: an ordinary, perhaps all too common, human experience is revelatory of something larger. What that larger insight or insights might be is naturally a source of disagreement. My current argument not only engages that disagreement, but also suggests that, for too much of the literature, the focus of analysis is likely to be misplaced. The question is not so much "How is it that I come to be bored, and what does it mean that I am?" The real question is, rather "Who is this 'I' imagined to be the subject of boredom, and how did its existence come to be presumed in just this way?"

This is one reason why the typical response of blaming the victim (or addict) is so out of place when it comes to the interface. As Michael Schulson has pointed out, comparing online addiction to gambling, "Overwhelmingly, the academic literature on gambling has focused on the minds and behaviors of addicts themselves. [Yet] there's something in between the gambler and the game—a particular human-machine interaction, the terms of which have been deliberately engineered."[8] Moreover, as he notes in discussing Natasha Schüll's 2012 book *Addiction by Design*, interaction has been structured by hundreds of very clever people whose main goal is to capture and hold your attention—even as we keep blaming you, the individual, for surrendering it. "In short, it's not exactly a fair fight," he writes. "When you read enough articles about internet compulsion and distraction, you start to notice a strange pattern. Writers work themselves into a righteous fury about prevalence and potency of addict-like behaviors. They compare tech companies to casino owners and other proprietors of regulated industries. And then, at the peak of their rage, they suggest it's the users—not the designers—who should change."[9]

Why not regulation, after all? Levy, in discussing addiction as a failure of extended agency, notes tellingly that individual selves have limits in their ability to exercise control over wayward desires. "[U]nified selves are a result, at least in important part, of negotiation, bargaining, and strong-arm tactics employed by subpersonal mechanisms as they attempt to achieve their ends," he writes, echoing the notion of mind divided against itself that is at least as old as Plato.[10] Now, as any addict knows, one can become habituated to all the twists and turns of one's own tactics—the subtle postponements, the bargaining, the false promises, and broken oaths. This, in fact, is what addiction actually feels like; that is why the psychology of addiction is so consistent across such different classes of stimuli (drugs, alcohol, tobacco, food, gambling, sexual promiscuity, work, violence, etc.). And so, in a more Aristotelian twist, these tactics are understood to be environmental as well as individual. "Addicts are too fragmented for normal attention-distraction techniques to have much chance of succeeding; instead they are most successful when they structure their environments so that the cues which remind them of theirs drugs are entirely absent."[11] Such structuring raises the opportunity-cost of the drug (via isolation or medication that induces a negative reaction), or it changes their relationship to their desire-driven discount curves (offering rewards for time spent abstaining or regular fellowship meetings in which to celebrate abstention).

Bolstering such mechanisms are more obvious extra-personal environmental controls such as price regulation, criminal levies for possession, bans on use in certain times or places, family/peer pressure, and organized social disapproval. We could add here such things as suicide fences (forcing a pause for reflection) and advertising campaigns (heightening unplanned awareness of harms). These external mechanisms all constitute forms of scaffolding by which agent-harmful desires are not obliterated, but rather rendered excessively costly—if only temporarily—so that the urge to satisfy is overpowered. By the same token, descaffolding conditions that offer easy access to stimuli, especially when combined with other factors that compromise full autonomy such as poverty, family dysfunction, or genetic predisposition, makes self-control that much more difficult to execute. (Note that some mechanisms, particularly family/peer pressure, are ambidextrous in this regard.)

Levy may still be too individualistic in his view, however. "Self-government, like political government, requires a monopoly on the coercive powers of the agent."[12] But perhaps, this is not so; after all, the achievement of a flourishing self, with will extended over time, might be counted as a public good. We want fully (if not ideally) autonomous agents for all kinds of familiar social reasons: to be good citizens, good parents, productive members of the cultural sphere, and so on. Surely, there is a stake in structuring the social environment that goes beyond coercive self-control, as powerful as that can be under ideal conditions.[13] This extension beyond isolated individual desires and actions is, indeed, the presumed rationale of "sin taxes" and substance control regulations of all kinds. Would such mechanism not be appropriate to the forms of autonomy impairment associated with the interface, even if we hold off the conclusion that such immersion is a case of full-blown addiction?

Schulson believes so, at least tentatively. He advocates greater control over a user's experience of the interface, especially with regard to the basic experience: regulating notifications and advertising, for example. More radically, perhaps there is a case for banning certain features of "compulsive design," such as Facebook's endless scroll of the dating apps' swipe function. In addition, heavy or obviously compulsive users of certain interfaces are easily identifiable using existing preference-monitoring algorithms. There could be triggers that "time out" users, post alerts, or cut-off access to given sites. Such mechanisms are already available on the self-control side of the ledger, blocking access to social media according to a previously posted limit. This is, in effect, a use of extended agency to reinforce a weaker self from the (prior) position of a stronger one. Perhaps, some interfaces themselves demand such a feature as a condition of access. More radical regulation is also possible, for instance, by limiting all forms of access according to set times and central controls. These would be highly unpopular, but we should note that virtually everything we know as feeding harmful desire is regulated in some such agent-external function, from outright criminality to liquor licensing and limited opening hours. Even foodstuffs must now carry labels indicating the precise breakdown of their ingredients.

The other obvious route of improvement in this quarter is the rise of "ethical design." If we stop blaming users for their engagement with various interfaces, yet maintain that such engagement is harmful, it follows that designers—like purveyors of drugs, fast food, prescription pharmaceuticals, or gambling venues—have certain special responsibilities. These might include, first of all, a sense that design ethics is a concern separate from profit margin or responsiveness to shareholders—that, indeed, social media and other forms of technological scenes are public goods.[14] More concretely, Joe Edelman has argued that we can use the traditional insights of economic choice theory to demonstrate that many of the (designed) choices on social media are harmful ones, "regrettable and isolating," in his words.

These harms can be addressed by more conscious menu design, allowing for greater freedom of choice—and hence possible goods that do not threaten autonomy—even as a public database of menus, choices, and outcomes could be compiled to track the evidence. (One current limiting feature of these debates is that most of the "evidence" amounts to anecdotal accounts, usually framed in unhelpful pro or con terms.) Such a database would put on record the hidden costs and false promises that are all too common among existing interface designs, allowing us to judge their alignment—or otherwise—with our informed and beneficial desires.[15]

There is, to be sure, a rival view, specifically on the issue of boredom. Many urban designers hold the conviction—often but not always unexamined—that boredom is always bad for those who experience it. In an effort to minimize stress, they advocate eliminating the occasions for boredom in, say, a street or park. Lack of interesting sights or stimuli pushes the brain into a condition of stress, such that individuals in the condition are more likely to engage in risky behavior to eliminate it. Thus, in a tricky extension of the neoliberal account of boredom, an argument is advanced that alleviating boredom counts as a public good, or at least an important goal in design. The assumption here is that stress is always bad, something to be eliminated as quickly as possible.

Now, far be it from me, as someone influenced by Rem Koolhaas and Jan Gehl, to advocate against better street design; but there are some large gaps in the line drawn from principles of good design to a general program of constant stimulus. Gehl, for example, following the classical thinking, argues for variety, not stimulus; this must include, crucially, those periods or stretches of the landscape in which we are understimulated, even bored by being so, such that (a) our thoughts may process the stimulus experienced before and (b) savor the potential renewal of stimulus at some future point. And, while nobody would argue in favor of needless suffering, there is a danger, I think, in viewing all unpleasant experiences as ones to be avoided at all costs. Sometimes, being understimulated is a good thing in and of itself. (This is distinct, I think, from the religious understanding of boredom as a frustrated underemployment of one's powers of thought and action—what Erich Fromm called a "paralysis of our productive powers.")[16]

The design writer Colin Ellard even notes a connection with addictive behavior of just the sort discussed earlier: "[R]esearchers discovered that even brief boring episodes increased levels of cortisol, which fits well with other recent suggestions that there could actually be a relationship between boredom and mortality rates," he writes. "Boredom can also lead to risky behavior. Surveys among people with addictions, including substance and gambling addictions, suggest that their levels of boredom are generally higher, and that episodes of boredom are one of the most common predictors of relapse or risky behavior."[17]

Ellard concludes with a sort of half concession concerning boredom. "When the external world fails to engage our attention, we can turn inward and focus on inner, mental landscapes. Boredom, it has sometimes been argued, leads us toward creativity as we use our native wit and intelligence to hack dull environments," he notes. "But streetscapes and buildings that ignore our need for sensory variety cut against the grain of ancient evolutionary impulses for novelty and will likely not lead to comfort, happiness or optimal functionality for future human populations." And, lest you be wondering, yes, there is an app for that: properly equipped, your phone can tell you when you are bored—just in case it was not obvious to you as, well, yourself. According to the *MIT Technology Review*, "A group of researchers say they've developed an algorithm that can suss [your level of boredom] out by looking at your mobile activity, considering factors like the time since you last had a call or text, the time of day, and how intensely you're using the phone."[18]

With this, the neoliberal argument has come full circle: boredom is induced by an environment; it is experienced by an individual as stress; the stress must be relieved; and addictive behavior is a possible version of the cycles of relief. Worst of all, this is evolutionarily hardwired into us! Therefore, we must do everything we can to limit boredom in the first place. But let us call out the social and political assumptions in play more clearly. Novelty in itself may answer some parts of our hardwiring, but it is not in itself a good. Moreover, boredom can be experienced under any circumstances, sometimes, especially those where there is a great deal of stimulation and easy, short-term satisfaction of desire. Boredom is the symptom, not the disease. To assume otherwise is merely to fall prey, once again, to the neoliberal account of the self.

No doubt, the debates on these points will continue. Let us simply remember that in the back of all such efforts and the political arguments about them lies the issue of the globally autonomous self, something we must continue to view with a skeptical eye. Not coincidentally, there is another Kafka resonance here. The late novelist David Foster Wallace, discussing the peculiar character of Kafka's humor, noted how hard it was for him to convey the comical quality of such apparently dark works to his American students. The problem, Wallace said, was that Kafka's humor did not fit any of the obvious categories that the students already had in hand. It was not satirical, or ironic, or slapstick, or sentimental.

It was, instead, something deep and forbidding, yet altogether familiar because human. In Kafka, we meet ourselves, as if through a glass darkly. Josef K, accused and convicted of crimes neither he nor we understand, helps his hapless executioners figure out how to wield the knife that will end his life. The man before the apparently locked door to heaven, in his derangement, begins conversing with the fleas in the collar of his tormentor's coat (the door has been unlocked the whole time). The humor here, Wallace argues, is not something you "get," the way you get a joke. His students are baffled because "we've taught them to see humor as something you get—the same way we've taught them that a self is something you just have."

No wonder, then, they cannot appreciate the essential Kafka joke, a species of irony at once comic and tragic: "That the horrific struggle to establish a human self-results in a self whose humanity is inseparable from that horrific struggle. That our endless and impossible journey toward home is in fact our home."[19]

Precisely! We will not confront this fact, and thus never appreciate the complexity of achieving selfhood at all, let alone effortlessly, as a mere presupposition if we are forever in the condition so vividly described by T. S. Eliot in "Burnt Norton": "Neither plenitude nor vacancy. Only a flicker / Over the strained time-ridden faces / Distracted from distraction by distraction / Filled with fancies and empty of meaning." Boredom is the symptom, not the diseases. Insofar as we concentrate on banishing it, or sublimating it into creativity or further consumption, we merely postpone—perhaps indefinitely—a confrontation with self that is essential to self. And an endless and impossible journey may well be often boring; it is nevertheless the journey upon which all of us are embarked.

Savoir Attendre

The positive account of selfhood we must offer in light of this critique— a defense of aesthetic contemplation and savoir attendre—forms a second stage of the critical work associated with the interface. I offer it here as an outline, not more, of schemes of resistance to the prevailing position that boredom must always be slayed or appeased. We can see in this positive proposal not a defense of boredom, still less another routine call for users to wean themselves of their devices or give them up altogether. The latter are now so common a feature of the discourse that they have generated their own subgenre of pushback critique, wherein people assert their rights to multitask, be shallow, and stimulate themselves at whatever level they choose.[20] (From both a philosophical and a psychoanalytic perspective, such people may simply be engaged in ever more articulate forms of denial.)

No, this is instead a kind of everyday politics of refusal, not just of consumption and its imperatives—about which so much has already been written—but also of the depredations on the self which can be registered here. I think all the various commentators would agree that extending the self over time (to use that language) is no mean feat. To achieve a self at all, one relatively stable and free of crippling addictions or routine tangling of desire, is also a tall order. Boredom is not the enemy here, contrary to what the neoliberal orthodoxy would have you believe. I might even put it in more hortatory fashion: trust your desires when they stall on you, just as you would trust that a stalled engine is a sign of deeper trouble. Feeding the bored self more stimuli, in hopes that that will solve the problem, is like grinding ignition again and again even as you flood the engine. And blaming the car for its failure can only lead to further frustration.

What is disanalogous in my image is that there is no solution to the problem of which boredom is a symptom. Perhaps, the biggest mistake we make, and do so repeatedly, is believing that there is some sort of repair shop for the self's breakdowns. There is not. (Sorry.)

Art is not the only form of savoir attendre, nor even perhaps the most obvious. But, for my purposes, it offers the ideal combination of reflection upon the nature of medium with an implied, sometimes demanded, imperative to contemplate. What can this mean? Consider a passage found toward the end of Guy Debord's *Society of the Spectacle* (*La Société du Spectacle*, 1967), in which the project of dismantling ideological presuppositions of consumable mediated experience generates the hint of a positive program. Debord notes that combatting comprehensive spectacular culture with the traditional tools of critical theory will only produce more confusion. In some cases, indeed, the tools of critical reflection will be commodified by the very targets they presume to strike. "Par là le délire s'est reconstitué dans la position même qui prétend le combattre [Thus, madness reappears in the very posture which pretends to fight it]," Debord cautions. "Au contraire, la critique qui va au-delà du spectacle doit savoir attendre [Conversely, the critique which is to go beyond the spectacle must know how to wait]."[21] Savoir attendre has multiple connotations we can fold together: not only patience, but also sometimes a kind of tactical readiness, an awareness that the ripeness is all. In some instances, there is a distinct religious overtone. We do not wait in vain, but it is possible we do not know quite what we are waiting for.

In arguing for the importance of art as a way of making subjects learn to wait, I am not suggesting that there is intrinsic superiority in "traditional" forms of creation or reiterating the discredited view that the contemplation of beauty is good for the soul. Nor am I falling into the too common denunciation of new media by reference to the terms of older ones. All media were, at some point, new. There is nothing new about newness! Instead, I want to focus on the specific ability of artistic media to reflect upon themselves. Generalizations about art are always risky and subject to immediate counterexample, but I enter this one with full awareness of the costs: art is the creation of objects or experiences that enable reflexive engagement with the conditions of that creation. A more familiar version of this claim is the traditional notion of aesthetic distance. We know that the scene upon the stage is not real or that the oil on the canvas represents a bunch of grapes rather than being one. That knowledge is of a special kind, afforded by the work itself, which is compatible at the very same time with the suspension of disbelief necessary to enjoy the work.

Artistic media, then—absent such specific endgame trickery as trompe l'oeil—are as much about their platform as their content, to use updated terms. In contrast to the media discussed at the beginning of this paper, the ones expressly designed to intertwine with neoliberal boredom, the interface of artistic media are explicitly present. The relationship of self to their demand for contemplative attention works only if this is so: we engage the interface, rather than allowing ourselves to be manipulated by it. An artwork might even be judged to fail if its interface slipped from view, rendering us (once again) mere consumers of our own selfhood.

These conclusions should not come as a surprise. The self, after all, is also a reflexive function of its medium, in this case consciousness. We are who we are precisely because, like artworks, we have the capacity to reflect upon our own conditions of possibility, not merely consume them. And insofar as that capacity is impaired by our own (literal) devices and desires, we are complicit in erosions of the self. Given how fragile any self must be, how difficult its achievement, we should be at least the wary of these forms of self-depredation. More urgently still, we should see clearly the political stakes of environments which encourage a lack of reflection over an enlivening of it.

Self-control is always a value in human affairs, as is freedom of choice when it comes to engaging with all media, whether phone apps, artworks, or my own consciousness. But the baseline condition of possibility for choice is a (relatively) autonomous self. From this point of view, boredom, because it emphasizes the problem of having an active desire, is like physical pain: a warning sign to be heeded, not a merely disagreeable sensation to be anesthetized. When it comes to selfhood, we need genuine stimulants, not narcotics or—worse—constantly renewed analgesics. Contrary to initial appearances, boredom, when understood and valued properly, has a unique capacity to stimulate self-reflection.

When it strikes, resist the urge to swipe left. But do not settle either. Wait, pay attention, and watch yourself. There is no higher calling!

Notes

1. See, for example, "What Toronto singles love (and hate) about dating in the city," *Toronto Star* (February 9, 2016); http://www.thestar.com/life/relation ships/2016/02/09/what-singles-love-and-hate-about-dating-in-toronto.html. The "commodification" and "hollowing-out" of tech-based dating apps was mentioned by several people interviewed for this article. One single person quoted there predicted that "2016 should the year of dating off the grid." But there are microgenerational differences to be noted here, with the singles quoted in the article above mainly lying within a 25-plus demographic. They also live in a large city where other dating opportunities were possible (many of them mentioned preferring to meet new people in bars or through networks of friends). One early 2016 article on National Public Radio's online magazine noted that the use of dating apps by Americans between 18 and 24 years old had tripled since 2013, according to a Pew Research Center study. See Jennifer Ludden, "Do You Like Me? Swiping Leads To Spike In Online Dating For Young Adults," The Two-Way (February 11, 2016); http://www.npr.org/sections/thetwo-way/2016/ 02/11/466342716/do-you-like-me-swiping-leads-to-spike-in-online-dating-for-young-adults?utm_source=nextdraft&utm_medium=email.

2. Eddington's book, *The Nature of the Physical World*, based on his 1926–1927 Gifford Lectures, was published in 1935 (London: Macmillan). In it, he defends his controversial "idealist" view that "The stuff of the world is mind stuff." Benjamin quotes Eddington at length, saying "one can virtually Kafka speak" in his prose; see "Some Reflections on Kafka," in Hannah Arendt, ed., and Harry Zohn, trans., *Illuminations* (New York: Schocken), pp. 141–145, at pp. 141–142.

3. Neil Levy, "Autonomy and Addiction," *Canadian Journal of Philosophy* 36:3 (September 2006), pp. 427–447, at p. 432 and p. 431.

4. Ibid., p. 433.

5. Rosecrans, Baldwin, "Throw away your earbuds, boredom is good," *Los Angeles Times* (February 7, 2016); http://www.latimes.com/opinion/op-ed/la-oe-0207-baldwin-boredom-benefits-20160207-story.html.

6. See Sandi Mann and Rebekah Cadman, "Does Being Bored Make Us More Creative?" *Creative Research Journal* 26:2 (2014): 166. This article cites and summarizes most of the recent psychological literature on the topic. Its central conclusion: The evidence "suggests that boredom can sometimes be a force for good.

This means that it might be a worthwhile enterprise to allow or even embrace boredom in work, education, and leisure. On an individual basis, if one is trying to solve a problem or come up with creative solutions, the findings from our studies suggest that undertaking a boring task (especially a reading task) might help with coming up with a more creative outcome" (p. 171).

7. Adam Phillips, "On Being Bored," in *On Kissing, Tickling, and Being Bored: Psychoanalytic Essays on the Unexamined Life* (Cambridge, MA: Harvard University Press, 1993), p. 68.

8. Michael Schulson, "User behaviour," Aeon (Fall 2015); https://aeon.co/essays/if-the-internet-is-addictive-why-don-t-we-regulate-it. See also Natasha Schüll, *Addiction by Design: Machine Gambling in Las Vegas* (Princeton, NJ: Princeton University Press, 2012).

9. Schulson, ibid.

10. Plato's notion of the divided psyche runs throughout his work, but is especially vivid in *Republic* and *Phaedrus*; the latter dialogue includes, at 246a–254e, the celebrated image of the soul as a chariot with a rational driver attempting to guide two horses, one unruly and one spirited but inclined to nobility. A recent riff on the idea imagines the "individual" mind as the emergent property of a fractious internal committee meeting in which Sleep, Sugar, Water, Protein, and Alcohol (among others) compete for control of the subject's agenda as she moves into Q2 of unemployment. Hallie Cantor, "My Brain: The All-Hands Meeting," *New Yorker* (August 24, 2015); http://www.newyorker.com/magazine/2015/08/24/my-brain-the-all-hands-meeting.

11. Levy, "Autonomy and Addiction," p. 437 and p. 442.

12. Ibid., p. 443.

13. Self-control has lately generated a large academic and popular literature, much of it referencing the celebrated Stanford "marshmallow test," which explores the ability of children to defer gratification and relates that ability to other successful tactics of thought and action, including higher SAT scores and lower Body-Mass Index numbers. The most accessible account is Walter Mischel, *The Marshmallow Test: Mastering Self-Control* (New York: Little, Brown and Co., 2014).

14. See, for example, Tristan Harris, "The Need for a New Design Ethic," a TED Talk archived at http://www.tristanharris.com/the-need-for-a-new-design-ethics/.

15. Joe Edelman, "Human Values, Choicemaking, and Interface Designs" (July 2014); http://www.tristanharris.com/the-need-for-a-new-design-ethics/.

16. "I am convinced that boredom is one of the greatest tortures," he wrote in *The Dogma of Christ*. "If I were to imagine Hell, it would be a place where we were constantly bored." Fromm, *The Dogma of Christ* (New York: Holt, Rinehart & Winston Inc., 1955), p. 181.

17. Colin Ellard, "Streets with no game," Aeon (September 1, 2015); https://aeon.co/essays/why-boring-streets-make-pedestrians-stressed-and-unhappy.

18. Rachel Metz, "Your Smartphone Can Tell When You're Bored," *MIT Technology Review* (September 2, 2015); https://www.technologyreview.com/s/540906/your-smartphone-can-tell-if-youre-bored/.

19. David Foster Wallace, "Laughing with Kafka," *Harper's Magazine* (July 1998), pp. 23–27.

20. See Nicholas Carr, "Is Google Making Us Stupid? What the Internet Is Doing to Our Brains," The *Atlantic* (July/August 2008); http://www.theatlantic.com/magazine/archive/2008/07/is-google-making-us-stupid/306868. Compare Steven Pinker, "Mind Over Mass Media," *New York Times* (June 10, 2010); http://www.nytimes.com/2010/06/11/opinion/11Pinker.html?_r=0. This unhelpful (and increasingly uninteresting) dichotomous thinking about the self's relation to media continues. The more recent version of Carr versus Pinker is Turkle versus Maladay et al. See Sherry Turkle, "Stop Googling. Let's Talk," *New York Times* (September 26, 2015), in which the celebrated programmer and author decries the excess of screen time over face time; http://mobile.nytimes.com/2015/09/27/opinion/sunday/stop-googling-lets-talk.html?_r=0; and Matthew J.X. Malady, "The Useless Agony of Going Offline," *The New Yorker* (January 27, 2016), who makes the usual arguments in favor of his own sense of choice and what the internet offers his desire; http://www.newyorker.com/books/page-turner/the-useless-agony-of-going-offline. Turkle's views are further assessed by Jacob Weisberg in "Are We Hopelessly Hooked?" *New York Review of Books* (February 25, 2016); http://www.nybooks.com/articles/2016/02/25/we-are-hopelessly-hooked/. This essay examines her books *Reclaiming Conversation: The Power of Talk in a Digital Age* (New York: Penguin, 2015) and *Alone Together: Why We Expect More from Technology and Less from Each Other* (New York: Basic Books, 2015), as well as Joseph M. Reagle, Jr., Reading the Comments: Likers, Haters, and Manipulators at the Bottom of the Web (Cambridge, MA: MIT Press, 2016) and Nir Eyal and Ryan Hoover, *Hooked: How to Build Habit-Forming Products* (New York: Portfolio/Penguin, 2015).

21. Section 220. English translation is from Guy Debord, *Society of the Spectacle* (Kalamazoo, MI: Black & Red, 1983), no pagination.

CHAPTER THREE

Attention, Emotion, and Desire in the Age of Social Media

Khadija Coxon

For better or worse, our age of social media has profoundly affected our social lives. Some feel that social media enhances social life, instantly connecting us across space and time and instigating democratizing, equalizing, and otherwise progressive social transformations. Others believe that social media disintegrates social life, disconnecting us from reality and from face-to-face relationships. This essay is not about whether social media is good or bad: It is about the value of social life in the age of digital technology. How have digital technology and social life become so entangled?

Part of the answer is that attention, emotion, and desire have unique social functions in the age of social media. Social media operates according to an *attention economy*. Apps like Facebook, Twitter, Instagram, YouTube, Snapchat, and others revolve around built-in metrics of attention—Likes, Retweets, Followers, and so on—so that using social media apps is like playing a game of vying for attention points. As our scores get higher, our desire for attention points increases. When we value another person's opinion or want to express that we care about them, we pay them in attention points. At the same time, these apps use very sophisticated built-in mechanisms of social and emotional regulation, primarily to serve social media companies' competitive interests in the attention economy. Many of us now have unquenchable thirst for measurable quantities of attention, but at the same time yearn for social goods that are harder to measure, like authentic relationships. The attention economy has conferred such high value on the very idea of social life, it is now both a commodity and a symbol of pricelessness.

The Attention Economy of Social Media

The term "attention economy" was first used by Herbert Simon[1] to describe the elevated value of processing resources in situations of informational abundance. The term has resurfaced in recent media scholarship and cultural criticism, to describe situations in which people are saturated with demands to receive and give attention.[2] Following these scholars, I use "attention economy" to clarify the sense in which there are gains and/or losses to social life in the context of digital media. Both those who praise and those who lament the age of social media translate attention as currency.

Social Life as Circulation of Online Attention

There is a positive story about social media that valorizes many ideas about the social, especially those attached to public social life such as democracy, equality, community, and progress. At the same time, the positive narrative embraces entrepreneurs as icons and capitalism as an ideology. I loosely trace this narrative to the key node of social media, the northern California tech scene. On this point, I am influenced by recent scholarship on new media, especially Alice E. Marwick's[3] ethnographic study of the tech scene, which began in 2006, when Web 2.0 was named "person of the year" by *TIME* magazine, and ended in 2010. During the time that Twitter was new to tech insiders, Marwick lived amongst, socialized with, and interviewed tech workers who had either achieved or were striving toward success in the tech world. Especially interesting for our purposes is Marwick's observation that the ethos of this group reflects an ironic hybrid of politically progressive, countercultural utopian idealism and libertarian entrepreneurialism. If we see the positive story of social media in terms of this hybrid, we can make some sense of the fact that enthusiastic users of social media are apt to hold on the one hand that creating and distributing digital content for free is doing social good, and on the other hand that properly entrepreneurial creators and distributors will be financially and socially successful.

The mixture of values, described above, is difficult to analyze without thinking through at least some of the cultural history of the tech scene. In this and the next paragraph, I summarize some of Marwick's version of this history, not so much to claim accuracy for its details, but to highlight the *contingency* of the values embedded in the positive story of social media. Marwick's account is structured around various scenes in which, leading up to the emergence of the social media era, digital technology played a major role in American countercultural movements. Hackers— from the 1950s at MIT, to the 1970s Californian cyberhippie movement, and onward—promoted ideals of transparency and openness with the slogan "information wants to be free." DIY hippies, punks, and feminists of the 1980s and 1990s embraced hacker idealism and its technology, moving beyond small-scale circulation of self-published leaflets to the wider circulation of webzines. In the 1990s and early 2000s, anti-corporate and anti-war activists, along with journalists of color, framed the blogo-sphere as the new frontier of participatory media. These countercultural uses of digital technology were politically complicated on their own terms, but the relevant point is that these movements and their progres-sive values were intertwined with the northern Californian tech scene before the dot-com boom. Before the boom, Silicon Valley was home to the idea that computer networks could produce a kind of cyber-utopianism driven by members of the movements I have mentioned, the ideas of Mar-shall McLuhan, psychedelic drugs, the rave scene, and prominent ex-hippies like Timothy Leary and the former Grateful Dead lyricist John Barlow. Burning Man—the annual art village that bans money, operating on economies of gifting, bartering, and volunteerism—was an early meet-ing place for cyber-utopians and remains an ideological touchstone for the tech industry.

As Marwick indicates, many remnants of the values of cyber-utopianism were retained by Silicon Valley start-ups through the dot-com boom, but were reformatted to suit new entrepreneurial discourses. The tech workers Marwick interviewed, like cyber-utopians, expressed commitments to val-ues of self-actualization, creativity, and self-expression, as well as lofty aims to "change the world." But these new tech workers parsed realization of their values in terms of entrepreneurial success, largely identified with "dis-covering" a self-brand and "sharing" it. Self-actualization via successful self-branding is a matter of promoting oneself as a corporate entity, being read as "authentic," and achieving high scores on the standard metrics of status built into social media applications—Friends, Followers, Likes, and clicks. (Marwick reports that, according to tech workers, social media applications include quantitative metrics of status because engineers understand numbers better than subtle or nuanced social indicators.)

The positive story of social media reflects the ideologies of an odd set of bedfellows, contingently linked groups that have promoted apparently similar values with multiple meanings. While cyber-utopians and contemporary tech workers appear to endorse similarly progressive values, the latter increasingly gauge success in terms of measurable online attention to their personal brands. The new tech workers' version of the positive story of social media does not present online attention as a means to promote progressive values, but rather as the very realization of progressive values. By offering Facebook as a new site of social life, Mark Zuckerberg literally changed the world. He also has achieved an extraordinary level of self-expression and self-actualization by becoming a globally recognized brand.

I have attempted to suggest that the positive story of social media encapsulates a contingent set of values inherited by the northern California tech scene. I also want to suggest that the influence of the positive story of social media outside the tech scene involves wide-scale deployment of the idea of social life as circulation of attention amongst brandable personalities. This point finds easy support from entertainment, an industry with close geographical and financial ties to the tech industry. For example, the success of Miley Cyrus, a 20-something pop star who has won at least 58 music awards and sold nearly 16 million albums, is increasingly judged in terms of her impressive social media statistics. It is important to notice here that the value of social media attention tends to be largely quantitative. Cyrus has (inconsistently) admitted that she strategically courts social media attention, often by behaving in ways she can predict will be interpreted as disgraceful or crazy. Becoming the topic of a Twitter discussion, or even better yet a fight, amplifies celebrity, which in an attention economy can be an end in itself. But Cyrus's celebrity in the sphere of social media amounts to more than simply being the topic of bad press. She is notorious for using social media to interact with her fans, and, in contrast with her competitors in the pop music world, does not follow the standard elite celebrity model of establishing hierarchical distance from fans. Instead, she publicly makes statements such as the following: "None of my friends are famous and not because of any other reason than I just like real people who are living real lives, because I'm inspired by them."[4] Cyrus is sometimes criticized by the entertainment industry, which treats her blatant attention seeking as gauche and desperate. However, she is equally praised as a businesswoman who cleverly engages online attention to develop a distinctive personal brand and an impressive fan base.

The idea that being socially effective centrally involves strategically engaging online attention has by now spread far beyond the tech and entertainment industries. Online self-branding is now integral to most professional spheres. As many readers of this essay will recognize, it is now common among academics, especially those on the job market, to be heavily invested in their stats on academic versions of social media sites, such as academia.edu.[5] Moreover, there is now an academic public relations industry that teaches academics both how to brand themselves and how to manage their online identities.

Perhaps, the most interesting evidence of social life as online attention is that youth, people who rarely have direct financial or professional stakes in the economy of online attention, nonetheless participate in the economy on an expert level. Youth are largely responsible for an entirely novel genre of photograph, the selfie. This achievement not only is notable to the history of photography, it also marks the invention of a valuable commodity. Youth have deployed the selfie in ways that make *cool* a trait of devices like iPhone and applications like Instagram and Snapchat. Youth are inventors and marketers for the tech industry, but they are willing to be paid in attention in lieu of money or professional advancement. They make bare the fact that, for many of us now, online attention is a social good.

Social Life as Return to Offline Attention

There is also a negative story about social media, one that valorizes social life but, instead of focusing on public social activity, focuses on in-person relationships with family and close friends. This narrative suggests that social media degenerates apparently *real* relationships, by over-orienting users to virtual worlds. This set of themes and values is ostensibly less complicated to understand than the themes and values of the positive story of social media, perhaps because the negative story of social media is premised on what looks like a straightforward philosophical position: Real and virtual social worlds are different, and losing from the real for the sake of the virtual is a bad thing.

The negative narrative gets more complicated when we try to explain the basis for sharply distinguishing between real and virtual social worlds. Let us consider three possible explanations, all arguments typically made by proponents of the negative story of social media. First, there is the suggestion that real relationships are unmediated, while virtual relationships are mediated. This suggestion typically involves the claim that mediated relationships divide attention in ways that have damaging social effects. For example, describing interviews she conducted with teenagers about the effects of social media on their relationships, Sherry Turkle[6] indicates that many young people express loneliness and frustration in relation to their parents' constant attention to digital devices like smartphones. Second, there is the idea that real relationships involve face-to-face interaction, while virtual relationships do not. This suggestion is typically accompanied by the claim that, without face-to-face interaction, we preclude attention to the kinds of subtle and nuanced social and emotional cues that define human communication and connection. Third, there is the idea that real relationships are grounded in joint attention to shared experiences of space and time, while digital space makes us spatially and temporally disconnected. Concerns about this kind of disconnection are now widely circulated via visual images of apparently disaffected people in the same physical space, who are intensely focused on screens as opposed to shared environmental stimuli. For example, in October 2015, a viral video posted to Reddit depicted a group of women at an Arizona Dimaondbacks game who appeared more focused on taking selfies than anything else.[7] The video features mocking and apparently angry commentary by sportscasters: "Every girl in the picture is just locked into her phone . . . welcome to parenting in 2015 . . ." and "The beauty of baseball is you can sit next to your neighbor and have a conversation . . . or you can completely ignore them." The indignation expressed in these comments is easy to relate to, because the women's behavior fails to recognize a significant cultural tradition of treating sporting events as sites of intense emotional contagion in the face of shared environmental stimuli.

Without rejecting the possibilities mentioned above, I point out that there are potential responses to all of them. First, with respect to worries about mediated relationships and divided attention, it is not clear that there was a golden age of relationships based on undivided attention before the digital age. The social media generation is not only not the first to complain of lack of attention from parents, it is the same generation associated with the term "helicopter parents"—parents who by definition pay too much attention to their children. It is at least logically possible that, in the context of an attention economy, wealth begets hunger for more wealth. Second, face-to-face contact cannot be a defining feature of offline relationships, because there are many online platforms that enable face-to-face contact, such as Skype and FaceTime. Members of YouTube microcommunities tend to focus heavily on facial and otherwise embodied communicative cues, to the extent that they often regulate each other's emotions by posting videos that highlight and respond to the subtle communicative cues expressed by other community members. Third, at least some online relationships are premised on joint attention to shared experiences. For example, members of online video game communities can only operate in contexts of joint attention to a shared goal, and will point out and reprimand perceived lack of attention to the goal.

Not long ago, before the social media age, critics worried that the television era was degenerating the value of art by reorienting audiences from live theatres to televisions.[8] These days, critics worry that social media is degenerating the value of social life by reorienting families and friends from communal activities (including television watching) to the digital spheres of smartphones, tablets, and laptops.[9] Both these sets of worries are about real losses. Even so, it is possible to read both sets of worries in terms of a singular genre of suspicion about mediation, which is premised on the idea that new forms of mediation undermine apparently timeless and universal principles, as opposed to our historically and culturally contingent values.

Competing Narratives of Social Life in an Attention Economy

The point of this section is *not* to defend or undermine either the positive or the negative story of social media. Both contain important insights. The point is that both narratives can be read as byproducts of the same attention economy. Just as the positive story of social media parses social gains in terms of attention, the negative story of social media parses social losses in terms of attention. Taken together, the narratives situate online and offline social life in direct competition with one another.

The positive and negative stories function as more than evaluative interpretations of digital technology and social media. They offer competing heuristics for how to spend in an attention economy and deploy the idea of social life as both a commodity and as a symbol of pricelessness. An interesting aspect of this competition is that the positive story tends to identify social life with what look like public relationships, and the negative story tends to identify social life with what look like private relationships. It thus might be tempting to read competition between the two narratives as an argument about public versus private social life. While I find this idea interesting, it lacks significant nuance. Many offline sites of social life are public spaces (e.g., parks, community centers, libraries, etc.). Moreover, social media users are not straightforwardly rational critics of a public sphere. They are consumers of products that are strategically designed to optimize consumer behavior. I will expand on this point in the next section.

Social and Emotional Regulation by Design

> Founded in 2004, Facebook's mission is to give people the power to share and make the world more open and connected. People use Facebook to stay connected with friends and family, to discover what's going on in the world, and to share and express what matters to them.
>
> —Facebook's mission statement

> The reason we did this research is because we care about the emotional impact of Facebook and the people that use our product. We felt that it was important to investigate the common worry that seeing friends post positive content leads to people feeling negative or left out. At the same time, we were concerned that exposure to friends' negativity might lead people to avoid visiting Facebook.
>
> —Facebook Scientist Adam Kramer on 2012 mood manipulation study

Social media companies are invested in their users' social interactions and emotions. As Facebook's mission statement illustrates, social media products are branded to deploy particularized versions of the positive story of social media. Companies like Facebook thus depend on users to behave in ways that reflect their own branded versions of the positive story of social media. Moreover, social media companies increasingly wage their financial success as advertising brokers on consumers' emotions, in light of the economic theory that happy people are, among other things, better ad consumers.[10] For these reasons, social media products are carefully designed to regulate users' social interactions and emotions.

Facebook's technological emotion management strategies offer a case study of *social and emotional regulation by design*. Social and emotional regulation by design is a counterexample to the negative narrative's implied premise that social media is (merely) a destructive force around a (more natural) state of offline social life. Social and emotional regulation by design offers evidence that digital technology has the capacity to generate new forms of social life, ones that involve apparently natural phenomena such as emotional experience and expression. Although this discussion criticizes the negative narrative, it is not a defense of the positive narrative. As the discussion will show, new forms of digital social life are dangerous: They function as instantiations of the values of the positive narrative, but we can reasonably read them as perversions of those values.

The case of Facebook suggests that social media spaces reshape users' understandings of self-expression and self-actualization, willing users voluntarily to infantilize themselves in the service of social media companies' efforts to accumulate attention.

Facebook's formal commitment "to give people the power to share" represents values of openness and community, and its suggestion that the platform enables users to "share and express what matters to them" represents values of self-expression and self-actualization. Facebook's brand is characterized by friendliness, positivity, fun, light heartedness, and optimism. For this reason, Facebook needs to ensure that its online communities cultivate traits of openness and community, and avoid the opposing traits of antagonism and negativity associated with brands like Reddit. In early 2012, Facebook gathered a team of special experts to design what would become Facebook's own brand of emoticons. The point was to prevent users from engaging in negative online social interactions, such as making mean comments and fighting. In some cases, negative social interactions on Facebook lead users to complain to administrators or even to "drop out," formally or informally. Negative social interactions also undermine Facebook's brand.

Facebook's integration of branded emoticons into its platform is a social regulation strategy, driven by a hypothesis about the management of human psychology: Typically, we rely on emotional cues of face-to-face contact to manage our social interactions, but on Facebook's hypothesis, these cues can be functionally replaced by online architectural mechanisms. In April 2013, the Facebook status update box began to include its "How are you feeling?" prompt, which leads to a dropdown menu of Facebook-branded emoticons. The mechanism acts as a reminder to users to translate their bodily emotional cues into digital ones. However, the mechanism does not entrust users with all or even most of the task of identifying and interpreting their emotions. Instead, the mechanism provides a discrete set of symbolic resources for affective expression, which are packaged to align with the fun, friendly, and lighthearted approach to self-expression and community that defines Facebook's brand.

The team that designed the emoticons included some notable personalities. One was Matt Jones, a story artist who works with the computer animation subsidiary of Disney, Pixar. Jones's illustrations are not realistic or artistically interesting, but his personal brand is associated with friendliness, lightheartedness, and cuteness, traits also aligned with Facebook's brand. Another personality was Dacher Keltner, a psychology researcher, former student of the influential American emotions researcher Paul Ekman, and Founding Co-Director of the Greater Good Science Center at the University of California at Berkeley. The Greater Good Science Center is a hub of researchers and other professionals who promote positive psychology, an area of psychology that focuses on well-being as opposed to psychopathology. Keltner's views on emotions are shaped by his membership in this distinctively Californian community of psychologists, which is driven by Westernized neo-Buddhist ideals of compassion, and which endorses Ekman's neo-Darwinian view that emotions are a universal and discrete set of biologically basic communicative cues. Keltner's scientific authority has been presented as evidence that the new emoticons are distinctively "authentic."[11] I point out that, although Keltner's understanding of emotions is not controversial in popular culture or in his home discipline of psychology, many researchers outside the discipline of psychology would reject his approach. Anthropologists of psychology since Lutz[12] have tended to view emotions as artifacts of culture, as opposed to basic universals. Philosophers of emotion remain divided on the issue of whether emotions are more or less cultural or more or less biological.[13] And although Keltner's approach reflects the dominant consensus view of emotions within academic psychology, the work of Lisa Feldman Barrett is an example of psychology research that rejects his brand of emotions theory.[14] It is worth asking why Keltner is an appropriate designer for Facebook. I suggest that it is, first, because his authority as a scientist employed by an elite institution *makes* the emoticons symbols of "authentic" emotional expression, and, second, because his approach complements Facebook's brand.

In September 2015, Mark Zuckerberg announced in a filmed speech that Facebook intended to respond to users' longstanding request for a "Dislike" button.[15] Zuckerberg was clear that there would not actually be a "Dislike" button, but rather a different kind of alternative to Facebook's tool to give "thumbs up" responses to other users' posts. Zuckerberg claimed that what users *really* want is a tool for expressing empathy, a mechanism for acknowledging other users' posts when a Like would be inappropriate (e.g., when another user posts about the death of a relative or posts a link to an article about a tragic event). In October 2015, Facebook executives announced that the new tool will involve another set of Facebook-branded emoticons—a heart, an angry face, a sad face, and a "wow!" face—which will appear as options in a dropdown menu when users hover over the Like button.[16] At the moment of this announcement, Facebook reiterated its claim that users do not want an opportunity to give "thumbs down" responses—users do not want opportunities to be mean—but rather want resources to express empathy or sympathy.

Zuckerberg's claim that users really want to express empathy, as opposed to mean and shallow feelings, was not immediately obvious to

Facebook users. His announcement was embedded in an online article on Facebook's website, and it was also the topic of numerous other online articles, most of which bore clickbait headlines about Facebook's intention to respond to requests for a "Dislike" button. In order to learn that there would be no "thumbs down" button, readers needed to move past the headlines of the articles. A week after the announcement, the online version of a popular Canadian magazine published a listicle titled "10 Posts You Can't Wait to Dislike on Facebook #Truth," which was prefaced by the statement "Sometimes you come across a post that really merits a giant eyeroll of dislike. These are those posts. Enter the newly promised Facebook Dislike button!" Clearly, the author had not read past the headlines of the articles about Zuckerberg's announcement or watched the video of his announcement. The fact that paid journalists do research without reading past headlines and refer their readers to articles they have not read is perhaps a symptom of operating within an attention economy.

The listicle was based on a poll of Facebook users, and it reflects the fact that at least some users relish even imagined opportunities to experience off-brand emotions. It is difficult to know how to evaluate this situation. On the one hand, social media users sometimes seem to resist digital social and emotional regulation strategies, but on the other hand, the resistance in this example is fairly banal. The poll's respondents, and the author of the article, resent spending attention on annoying online content, but their way of expressing their resentment is to spend more attention on their resentment in an online forum.

For many of us now, it seems almost inevitable that our online environments will modulate our emotions. This became especially evident in the aftermath of the publication of a now infamous mood manipulation experiment by the Facebook scientist Adam Kramer and psychologists from Cornell and University of California.[17] The experiment was conducted in 2012 and involved deliberate manipulation of the algorithms of 700,000 newsfeeds, so that users saw either an exceptionally high amount of negative content or an exceptionally high amount of positive content. The results of the experiment indicated that Facebook's newsfeed algorithms can be designed to produce a kind of mediated emotional contagion, which motivates users to post more positive content when they are exposed to more positive content (or the reverse). The study would not have been revealed to the public, if not for the fact that a report of it was published in *Proceedings of the National Academy of Sciences* (*PNAS*).[18] At that moment, Facebook was accused, mainly by academics, of failing to follow standard academic norms of informed consent. While *PNAS* published an editorial letter of concern, admitting that the study's authors had breached norms of research ethics, and Facebook executive Sheryl Sandberg admitted that the study was "poorly communicated," it became evident that it is regular practice for tech companies to treat users as a free pool of unknowing research subjects.[19] While some commentators predicted the incident would result in broad loss of trust in the Facebook brand, it is not clear whether hypothetical or actual losses of trust have had significant material effects on Facebook. The event may not have made a point about Facebook in particular, so much as a more general point about the friendly surveillance culture of social media.

In popular media accounts, the public's discomfort about the mood manipulation experiment was almost entirely framed around the issue of breach of academic norms of informed consent. This framing is somewhat misleading, because it does not acknowledge that the most common word used in critical reactions to the event was "creepy." It is unsettling to acknowledge that we voluntarily spend much of our lives in environments with built-in mechanisms of social and emotional control. But it is difficult to discern how much danger to read into online surveillance, especially when what makes it creepy is its resemblance to Kindergarten pedagogy. Besides, we all understand that Facebook's warmly packaged social and emotional regulation mechanisms are strategies to compete for attention. In an attention economy, perhaps even creepy strategies are fair game.

Desire as Social Aspiration

If the positive and negative stories of social medias operate according to an attention economy, we might wonder what attention can buy: What are the objects of desire that drive the attention economy of the digital age? The positive story of social media often focuses on the idea that those who earn enough online attention achieve *fame*, a level of success attached to entrepreneurial self-actualization, while the negative story of social media often nostalgically implies that those who pay enough attention to offline relationships return to more *authentic* ways of living and relating to others. In this section, I suggest that these presentations of fame and authenticity are prompts to desire the pursuit of a better social self. I call this kind of desire "social aspiration." As I will illustrate, social aspirations of the digital age often blend the values of the positive and negative stories of social media, constructing fame and authenticity as intertwined social ends, and making social life a salient field of desire.

During the 1970s and 1980s, media scholars treated the media as an instrument of the state or capital, which mediated or translated these institutions' interests into cultural symbolism. However, some scholars now suggest that, since the early 2000s, the media has become driven primarily by its own (commercial) interests and is now more an author than a mediator of culture.[20] Central to this argument is the observation that imagery around celebrity has shifted, from the elite to the ordinary. As Laura Grindstaff and Susan Murray[21] have argued, new media presents the idea of celebrity as attainable to ordinary people at a historical moment of downward social mobility, unemployment, and economic instability. Graeme Turner[22] frames this shift as a *demotic turn*, emphasizing the Greek root of democracy, *demos*, which refers to common people. Not only is celebrity now a common pursuit of ordinary people, recent research indicates that increasing numbers of young people now think of fame *per se*—fame not as a byproduct of some activity or talent, but fame in itself—as a career option.[23]

Social media companies have financial and rhetorical interests in the aspirations to fame of ordinary people. A significant function of applications like YouTube and Instagram is to distribute content made by and marketed to ordinary people. Thus, ordinary people are not only the target market of social media products, but also free to cheap laborers, self-styled as entrepreneurial content creators. I believe some social media content creators aspire to a particularly ordinary kind of fame, which is distinct from the elite fame of the celebrities typically featured in broadcast media (namely elite entertainers, politicians, and athletes). There are hierarchical distinctions between social media celebrity and elite celebrity, and the social media celebrities who are most well known outside the sphere of the Internet are the few who manage crossover from ordinary to elite. For example, the story of pop sensation Justin Bieber's rise to fame typically begins at the moment when his popular YouTube videos were "discovered" by a talent scout with connections to the producers of elite celebrity musicians. From this point, Bieber's trajectory resembles the trajectories of teen pop stars of previous generations who were discovered on televised talent competitions and were turned into stars by the machinery of the pop music industry.

While social media attention is potentially an instrument to achieve ends like elite celebrity, some content creators desire ordinary fame as a social end in itself. Not unlike reality television stars, social media celebrities are often criticized for not having skills and talents associated with traditional, elite celebrity, such as acting or singing ability. This criticism highlights the fact that digital content creators face real barriers to crossing over to the sphere of elite celebrity. However, the criticism also misses the point that the phenomenon of ordinary celebrity reconstructs the meaning of fame. The elite celebrity is symbolized by the metaphor of the star, characterized by mystery and hierarchical distance and associated with naturalized qualities of talent and class. The ordinary celebrity attracts attention through regular and frequent interactions with other ordinary people. Achieving ordinary fame as a social media celebrity is like doing well at a game, because in this sphere, fame is nothing more nor less than relatively high scores on attention scales, the metrics of subscribers, followers, Likes, or clicks built into social media applications.

With over 16 million followers and over a billion clicks, Jenna Marbles operates the seventh most subscribed-to channel on YouTube and the most subscribed-to channel run by a woman. Her videos use sarcastic and self-deprecating humor to address themes of contemporary living as a young American woman. Marbles's first viral video, "How to trick people into thinking you're good looking,"[24] is a mock tutorial, which she claims is for people who are "born ugly, like me," and which provides a time-lapse, beginning-to-end depiction of her ordinary grooming practices (viz., hair, makeup, and wardrobe). At the beginning of the video, she seems plain, but by the end, her looks have radically transformed: She seems overtly sexual and is conventionally attractive, if not particularly "classy." Marbles provides running commentary, presenting her beauty rituals as fakery, and indicating desperation in her self-sexualizing: "Now it's time for eye makeup. I like to use colors like black, because it says, 'I'm a whore'. The goal is to make yourself look *nothing* like yourself." The video is quasi-satirical: Marbles is ridiculing and providing critical analysis of a certain type of ordinary woman in her twenties, while clearly embracing her identity as one of those women. This approach makes Marbles' fans describe her as "hilariously relatable."[25]

Marbles' fame comes with financial success: She is reportedly worth approximately US$2.5 million. Although Marbles is wealthier than most ordinary people, especially the young women who make up her target market, her financial success is not mind-boggling enough to establish hierarchical distance between her and her audience. Marbles films her videos in her home, an expensive suburban house that many ordinary North Americans might aspire to, which does not display design features, art objects, or decor that suggest refined taste or elite preferences. Given the nature of her videos, Marbles is arguably a comedian and part of the entertainment industry, but her wealth is just not comparable to the wealth of elite celebrity entertainers of the same age and gender. Pop singer Katy

Perry, for example, is reportedly worth approximately US$250 million. At the same time, within the sphere of social media, Marbles is objectively more famous than Perry: Quantitative metrics clearly indicate that Marbles is winning on scores of subscribers, followers, likes, and clicks.

In April 2013, Marbles and her success were the topics of an article in the *New York Times*, and soon after she was interviewed for a segment of the ABC news program *Good Morning America*. The segment was widely discussed by YouTube content creators who felt it had ridiculed Marbles and her work, dismissing the possibility that her success was based on skill, and treating her as a ditzy amateur. Marbles described the reporter as "ignorant of how this Internet machine works," and her fellow social media content creator Hank Green posted the following to his Tumblr page:

> And in the end, that's how the entire segment feels to me, a bunch of people making fun of a creator who they are threatened by and who they do not understand. And of course they're threatened by it, Jenna Marbles (on her own, with a cheap camera) can make a video that gets more [views] by more people than an episode of *Good Morning America*.[26]

These remarks suggest that social media content creators view themselves as skilled entrepreneurs, in direct competition for audience attention with broadcast media as opposed to amateurs trying to copy or become elite media figures.

When Turner[27] uses the term "demotic turn," he means to capture a duplicitous phenomenon: He argues that the media's turn to ordinariness implies democratizing activity in the absence of changes to the structure of political authority (*kratos*). Turner mainly applies this point to his analyses of reality television, and I think it has merit. However, the point is less straightforward in the case of the ordinary celebrity of social media. Jenna Marbles' fame is determined by votes from ordinary people, who subscribe to her channel, click on her videos, and follow her on Instagram, Twitter, and Facebook. So, social media content creators are right to point out that their ability to attract attention and accumulate fans is a threat to traditional broadcast media. Social media content creators have quite legible reasons for desiring the fame of ordinary celebrity and for feeling socially successful when they do. At the same time, I emphasize that it would be a mistake to think that social media content creators have achieved political dominance in the world of media. Digital content creators do not own their means of cultural production, and they provide either free or relatively cheap labor to the companies that do.

Marbles' high level of ordinary fame inspires social aspirations in other YouTube content creators, even ones who are not entertainers and who have no potential to cross over to elite celebrity. Marbles' ordinary fame is a model of entrepreneurial success that stands in contradistinction to the idea that conventional, 9–5 models of earning a living are the only options for obviously nonelite people. This model works especially well on YouTube, where microcommunities often converge around aspiring entrepreneurial microcelebrities. Take, for example, Freelee the Banana Girl and Durianrider, an Australian couple in their late thirties, who are micro-celebrities in an online microcommunity of health and fitness Vloggers. As the story goes, Freelee and Durianrider first came to the Internet at a time when both were homeless and surviving on welfare. Apparently, they used a computer at a public library to start a website they named "30 Bananas a Day,"[28] an old-fashioned discussion board for people interested in their very unconventional lifestyle, which revolves around eating a high-calorie, high-carbohydrate vegan diet, mainly in the form of raw fruit, and intensely participating in outdoor endurance sports like cycling and running. They claim that their intention was only to find a community of like-minded people, and at the time they had no aspirations to make money, let alone achieve fame.

Whatever their initial intentions, over time, Freelee and Durianrider have leveraged the attention economy of social media, especially YouTube, to build their lifestyle into a full-fledged brand. Some of their attention-seeking methods involve rhetoric that existed before social media. For example, like the protagonists of reality television shows like "The Biggest Loser" and "Intervention," Freelee and Durianrider each have a personal transformation story. Durianrider describes himself as a guy raised by a poor single mother who failed high school, did drugs, and committed petty crimes throughout his late teens and early twenties.[29] Freelee describes herself as a formerly overweight, depressed, and anxious yo-yo dieter.[30] Both frame conversion to their brand of vegan lifestyle as a turning point, which inevitably makes whoever follows it thin, fit, and fulfilled by the purpose of "saving the animals and the planet." They often cite this ideological mission as their motivation for being on YouTube and other social media sites, and claim they "don't care about the money."

Freelee and Durianrider also use attention-seeking strategies that are specific to social media. They post videos regularly and frequently. They interact with their audience, by posting video responses to prominent comments and questions and by trolling timely discussions in their community. Durianrider's brand centrally involves aggressively criticizing the latest activities of rival Vloggers to the ends of "dispelling the myths of the health and fitness movements" and "exposing snake oil tactics." Freelee and Durianrider repeatedly claim that they are transparent and authentic, often in comparative terms: "No one on the Internet besides us has the balls to tell it like it is." They show viewers where they live, how they spend their time, and how they spend their money. Viewers are given illustrations that the couple often goes to Thailand for extended periods, where they live cheaply and try to appreciate what they view as "real" poverty. Viewers also see that, in their home country of Australia, they tend to live in short-term, modest rental apartments and do not invest much money in things like furniture and clothing. At the same time, they demonstrate that they have achieved financial success from YouTube ad revenue, both by repetitively stating so, and by emphasizing that they are able to afford plane tickets, high performance cycling equipment, and notoriously, a weekly budget of several thousand dollars for organic fruit.

Freelee and Durianrider's ordinary fame is an inspiration to younger social media content creators in their community, who tend to be university-aged middle class women. One of them was Essena O'Neill, an Australian teenager who, from 2013 to 2015, became so good at commanding attention on YouTube and Instagram that she quit university after one year, claiming that social media promised a better future. Then, very suddenly in 2015, Essena had a public "meltdown," saying that for years she had been lonely and empty. She claimed she pursued high quantities of attention at the cost of living ethically and having emotionally satisfying relationships. She deleted all her social media accounts and encouraged others to take a stand with her. Unfortunately for Essena, her exit from social media had the opposite of its intended effect. For a few months, her story became a "trending topic"—it was discussed extensively by social media users and even very high-profile traditional media outlets.[31] Her name became a search engine optimization (SEO) keyword—social media content creators started to use her name in the titles of posts, in order to attract more attention. While some of the traditional media attempted to use Essena's story to start a discussion about the psychological difficulties young people face in the social media age, the topic fizzled out quickly. In the meantime, Essena has become an object of ridicule and disdain in her former social media community. Durianrider, who was formerly one of her biggest supporters, now refers to her pejoratively as "Queenie (the scene queen)"— someone who pursues the highest rung of the social ladder but is too immature to use her power effectively. He reads her story as one of failure to appreciate the "real" value of being able to command a lot of attention.

After O'Neil announced that she had quit university, some social media users accused Durianrider and Freelee of leading young people down a bad path. Durianrider responded in a video:

> It's a crazy lifestyle . . . social media . . . because how many people do you know who, any day of the year—any day—can wake up, and look at the ceiling and say "What do I want to do today?" Any day of the week, I can pick up my bike, chuck it in a box and fly anywhere in the world. Any day of the week. How many people do you know who can do that? That's the sort of freedom that I've worked for. I didn't have rich parents . . . I'm self-made, I'm not an estate-fund kid . . . I'm just saying that I'm self-made, so I'm self-passionate . . . I do it for the animals. I've travelled around the world . . . and this world is fucked up! So, I've got to get the message out there. . . . A lot of these young kids on social media . . . it's this perfection mindset, "Oh well my video's not too good, I'll zoom around and change the lighting," No! Just upload a fucking video. I don't want to hear your excuses! The animals don't want to hear your excuses! Work your ass off today, upload some content today. . . . No more excuses! And please, no more "you guys are bad examples." Look at our fucking lifestyle! Is that a bad example? If it is . . . get fucked! It's not your parents' reality![32]

Durianrider argues that young people now have the opportunity to achieve a unique kind of freedom through online social life, not in spite of their ordinariness, but precisely because of it. When he criticizes those who focus on making perfect videos, he is emphasizing the point that winning at social media involves accruing large quantities of attention and to do that requires putting out large quantities of content. He views those who, like Essena, lose focus on the endpoint of attracting attention as inauthentic, cowardly, and unethical.

Marbles, Durianrider, Freelee, and Essena have all achieved different levels of ordinary fame, which are nothing more than sums of attention. Each aim for different amounts and kinds of attention, but they all aspire to ordinary as opposed to elite celebrity. What is especially interesting for our purposes is that the ordinariness of their celebrity is at least sometimes also a way of achieving authenticity. This suggests that the values of the positive and negatives stories of social media are not as distinct as they first appear. Both the narratives urge us to desire to become better versions of our social selves, whether we pursue fame online, authenticity offline, or some amorphous hybrid of the two.

Conclusion

I have framed the positive and negative stories of social media as two threads of a singular narrative about social life, which now constantly asks us what it means to be in association with others and why our associations matter. This story is a marketing tool of our new attention economy, which sometimes presents social life as a commodity and sometimes makes it a symbol of pricelessness. These conflicting framings of social life circulate through our daily interactions with social media applications, they arise in our criticisms of these applications, and they sometimes converge through our desires. Instead of asking whether the digital age is strengthening or eroding social life, we might instead ask just what *social life* is and why it matters to us so much.

Notes

1. Herbert Simon, "Designing Organizations for an Information-Rich World," in *Computers, Communication and the Public Interest*, ed. M. Greenberger (Baltimore, MD: The John Hopkins Press, 1969), 32–71.

2. Alice Marwick, *Status Update: Celebrity, Publicity and Branding in the Social Media Age* (New Haven, CT: Yale University Press, 2013); Laura Grindstaff and Susan Murray, "Reality Celebrity: Branded Affect and the Emotion Economy," *Public Culture* 27, no. 1 75 (2015): 109–135; Graeme Turner, "The Mass Production of Celebrity: Celetoids, Reality TV, and the 'Demotic Turn,'" *International Journal of Cultural Studies* 9, no. 2 (2006): 153–165.

3. Alice Marwick, *Status Update: Celebrity, Publicity and Branding in the Social Media Age* (New Haven, CT: Yale University Press, 2013).

4. Sierra Marquina, "Miley Cyrus Doesn't Need a 'Squad' Like Taylor Swift, Has Normal Friends: 'I Just Like Real People,'" *US Weekly* (August 31, 2015).

5. Deborah Lupton, "'Feeling Better Connected': Academics' Use of Social Media." (Report published by News & Media Research Center, University of Canberra, 2014.)

6. Sherry Turkle, *Alone Together: Why We Expect More from Technology and Less from Each Other* (New York: Basic Books, 2011).

7. pnw_smalls, "Sorority Girls at a Baseball Game," *Reddit* (October 1, 2015).

8. Dennis Dutton, "Freedom and the Theatre of Ideas," Address to the Russian Institute of Aesthetics (January 1990).

9. Sherry Turkle, *Alone Together: Why We Expect More from Technology and Less from Each Other* (New York: Basic Books, 2011).

10. Will Davies, *The Happiness Industry: How Government and Big Business Sold Us Well Being* (London, UK: Verso Books, 2015).

11. Josh Constine, "Compassion Researcher Helps Facebook's Apps Get Emotional With Animated Stickers," *Tech Crunch*.

12. Catherine Lutz, *Unnatural Emotions*.

13. Ronald de Sousa, "Emotion," in *Stanford Encyclopedia of Philosophy*, ed. Zalta En.

14. Lisa Feldman Barrett, "Psychological Construction," *Emotion Review* 5 (2013): 379–389.

15. Facebook Newsroom, "Highlights from Q&A with Mark," (September 15, 2015).

16. Davey Alba, "Facebook Tests Emoji Reactions," *Wired* (October 8, 2015).

17. Adam Kramer, Jamie Guillory, and Jeffery Hancock, "Experimental Evidence of Massive-Scale Emotional Contagion through Social Networks," *Proceedings of the National Academy of Sciences* 111, no. 24 (2014): 8788–8790.

18. Ibid.

19. Gail Sullivan, "Sheryl Sandberg not sorry for Facebook mood manipulation study." *Washington Post* (July 3, 2014).

20. Graeme Turner, "The Mass Production of Celebrity: Celetoids, Reality TV, and the 'Demotic Turn.'" *International Journal of Cultural Studies* 9, no. 2 (2006): 153–165.

21. Laura Grindstaff and Susan Murray, "Reality Celebrity: Branded Affect and the Emotion Economy," *Public Culture* 27, no. 1 75 (2015): 109–135.

22. Graeme Turner, *Ordinary People and the Media: The Demotic Turn* (London: Sage, 2010).

23. Su Holmes, "All You've Got to Worry About Is the Task, Having a Cup of Tea, and Doing a Bit of Sunbathing: Approaching Celebrity in Big Brother," in *Understanding Reality Television*, ed. Su Holmes and Deborah Jermyn (London: Routledge, 2004), 111–135.

24. Jenna Marbles, "How to trick people into thinking you're good looking," YouTube video (July 9, 2010).

25. Jennifer McCall, "Marbles's Tweets are Hilariously Relatable"; Nico Lang, "45 Hilariously Relatable Jenna Marbles Quotes That Are Words to Live By." *Thought Catalog.*

26. Hank Green, quoted in Aja Romano, "Hank Green on why 'GMA' has Jenna Marbles all wrong," *The Daily Dot* (April 23, 2013).

27. Graeme Turner, *Ordinary People and the Media: The Demotic Turn* (London: Sage, 2010).

28. http://www.30bananasaday.com/.

29. Durianrider, "How I overcome suicidal depression," YouTube video (April 26, 2014).

30. Freelee the Banana Girl, "Anorexia, bulimia, Part 2 my recovery Freelee's story," YouTube video (May 17, 2012).

31. Jonah Bromwich, "Essena O'Neill, Instagram Star, Recaptions Her Life," *New York Times* (November 3, 2015); Elle Hunt, "Essena O'Neill quits Instagram claiming social media 'is not real life,'" *The Guardian* (November 3, 2015).

32. Transcribed and abridged, from: Durianrider, "Essena Oneill Quits Uni Cos of Us," YouTube video (June 21, 2015).

CHAPTER FOUR

Social Media and Self-Control: The Vices and Virtues of Attention

Juan Pablo Bermúdez

The vices and virtues of attentional self-control, the capacity to resist temptations and pursue longer-term goals over immediate gratifications, are crucial in determining the shape of our lives and our ability to form our identities. This capacity is intimately linked to our ability to control the direction of our attention. This raises the worry that perhaps social media are making us more easily distracted people, and therefore less able to exercise self-control. Is this so? And is it necessarily a bad thing?

The Web 2.0 and the Perils of Distraction

Picture a child sitting in front of a long, empty table. An adult in front of her—the only other person in the room—puts a marshmallow on the table, right in front of the child, and tells her she has two options: she could eat one marshmallow right now, or she could wait until the experimenter came back, and then she would get two marshmallows.

This is the setting of what has become one of the most famous psychological experiments. The children in the test are of preschool age (around 4.5 years old on average). In getting them to pick between a smaller, sooner reward and a larger, later reward, researchers sought to assess their capacity for self-control, that is, for postponing gratification and persisting in the search for a greater, more distant goal. The children had to wait typically 15 minutes in a lonely room designed to have no distracting elements, while avoiding a temptation that was, quite literally, in front of their faces.

While interesting on its own, the study became famous when researchers followed up on the original participants and assessed how they were doing during their adolescence and adulthood. They found that those who had managed to delay gratification as children were later more likely to have higher academic scores, more stable emotional lives, richer relationships, and lower Body Mass Indexes.[1]

So, it seems that the "marshmallow experiment"—as it is usually called—managed to measure a very crucial, multipurpose capacity that contributes greatly to the overall shape our lives take. Researchers found that the self-control capacities at stake here were correlated to children's ability to control their attention: those who were most successful in waiting for the bigger reward managed to keep their mind focused on things other than the marshmallow. To do this, they used mental tricks, like transporting themselves to other places with their imagination, or bodily tricks, like closing their eyes. Thus, there is reason to think that our capacity for controlling our attention and our capacity to exert self-control are very closely linked.

By "self-control," I refer to the capacity to select which among our desires and intentions become effective in our behavior, and follow through with that selection despite distractions and temptations. This amounts to the capacity to control ourselves, that is, to give shape and contour to our identities as agents through time. In this sense, self-control is very closely linked to notions like autonomy and freedom of the will. The ultimate philosophical teaching of the marshmallow experiment may therefore be that self-control, and this capacity to shape ourselves is heavily dependent on the capacity to control the direction of our attention.[2]

And this is why the recent emergence of social media may be worrisome. The rise of the Internet as the new dominant means of communication has tended to produce a massive increase in the average quantity of content we process every day, as well as in the speed at which we process it. Many are becoming concerned that such vertiginous increases in quantity and speed may be eroding our ability to keep our attention focused on a given object for any lengthy amount of time. Moreover, this erosion of attention seems to be taken further by the rise of the "Web 2.0" (the tendency to transform the Internet into a socially constructed medium by allowing users themselves to generate their own content through, e.g., profile construction, commenting and rating, liking or disliking, following or unfollowing, and so on), because now also our social identities are at stake in each new wave of content delivered in the form of a notification, a chat, a Facebook update, or comment. Anyone with some first-hand online experience has probably experienced what it is like to not be able to keep their attention in one place for much longer than a few seconds, due to the constant interruptions of the Web 2.0.

So, if the internet and social media are eroding our ability to control our attention, and if attentional control is crucial to self-control, we may justifiably worry about whether social media are undermining our ability to shape our own lives by making us less able to focus on our goals and more likely to chase after immediate diversions.

This is not the first time people have worried about the negative effects a new communication medium may have on the human mind. Plato, for one, was gravely concerned about the profoundly negative consequences of the great communication revolution of his age: writing. In the Phaedrus, he has Socrates tell the story of a great inventor who has just created the written word, who then presents it as a gift to the Egyptian king. To this, the king replies: "This discovery of yours will create forgetfulness in the learners' souls, because they will not use their memories; they will trust to the external written characters and not remember of themselves."[3] By fixating words into text, the truth of the ensouled speech will be reduced to the mere appearance of truth of the characters in the inert page. And, as dead records pile up, living memory will deteriorate.

Few people alive today would think that Plato was justified in his criticism of writing. Even if—as it surely was the case—we lost something irreparably by leaving the mind of the oral tradition behind, the possibilities opened by writing far outstrip any possible downsides it may have. Most of us would surely agree that illiteracy has proven to have much more paralyzing consequences than literacy. Yet, Plato had no way of foreseeing the new possibilities that would open up with the printing press and the democratization of reading and writing.

Something similar may be occurring to us: the appearance of digital media may be too close to our own time for us to truly envision the new possibilities it opens up. Still, Platonism has had a recent resurgence of sorts, inspired by the Internet and its social turn. If Plato's Socrates was worried that writing may deprive us of our memory and make us forgetful, defenders of what I call "Platonism 2.0" are now worried that the internet may be depriving us of our capacity for sustained attention and making us distracted. Nicholas Carr has recently produced a forceful defense of this strand of Platonism.[4] Against utopian views of the Web 2.0, Carr argues that the new media are "changing our brains" in ways that have unforeseen negative consequences: they erode our capacity for the paused, reflective concentration historically associated with the ascendance of the book, and replace it with an ever-increasing disposition toward superficial skimming and continuous skipping from one hyperlink to the next, from one e-mail to the next tweet to the new viral cat video.

Paradoxically, the Internet "seizes our attention only to scatter it," says Carr. "We focus intensively on the medium itself, on the flickering screen, but we're distracted by the medium's rapid-fire delivery of competing messages and stimuli." Support comes from studies suggesting that whereas reading a book activates mainly zones in the brain associated with memory, language, and vision, web browsing activates many more brain areas, particularly the prefrontal areas associated with decision-making. This may sound positive (the Internet makes us exercise more brain regions!), but it is the opposite: surfing the Web implies constantly making decisions (about which link to click on, whether to like or comment each post, etc.) and continuously shifting between tasks (navigating between a myriad browser tabs and program windows, which in turn house their own distinct choice problems); such increase in choice-making and multitasking leads to a cognitive overload, because it turns out we are not particularly good at either of those things (more on this below). Many of the basic technologies that make up the Internet as the specific medium it is impose decision-making and multitasking problems. Take the hyperlink:

> Whenever we, as readers, come upon a link, we have to pause, for at least a split second, to allow our prefrontal cortex to evaluate whether or not we should click on it. The redirection of our mental resources, from reading words to making judgments, may be imperceptible to us . . . but it's been shown to impede comprehension and retention, particularly when it's repeated frequently.

Thus, the Internet enables us to process more things, but it simultaneously spreads our attention much more thinly to cover a wider area of content and makes it continuously shift between tasks. This, in turn, implies that we end up processing each bit of content at much shallower levels than we could do before the hyperlink, when our minds were entirely focused on only following the linear content of a book. This is what Carr thinks the Internet is ultimately doing to us: turning us into shallower thinkers, taking away the capacity for deep, sustained concentration that the book medium had enabled us to perform.

Many feel that the Platonist 2.0 is making too much of a deal about the Internet's effects on our brains. After all, it is not like deep concentration is our authentic way of being, and that distraction and impulsiveness are essentially worse than it is. If what the Platonist is concerned about is that we may lose our authentic selves, then we would do well to remember that all our modes of being—including the book's lengthy concentration mode—are mediated by particular cultures and traditions, social environments, and communication technologies, none being more natural or authentic than another.[5]

But we should not underestimate the new Platonist's concern. For, as the marshmallow experiment has shown, what is at stake here is our ability to control the overall shape of our lives. Attentional control undergirds self-control, and self-control is necessary for successfully resisting temptation and following the path we have chosen for ourselves. If the Web 2.0 is making us more distracted, then it may well be depriving us of our ability to control our lives and surrendering it to the external forces that we happen to come across.

But what is the evidence for that claim? And if it is true, would it really be a bad thing? Or could it be the opportunity for the emergence of new kinds of skills and identities that go beyond what the book has allowed?

I will try to answer these questions by exploring what we currently know about the effects of social media on attention and self-control. The issue is more complex than it may seem, and there is reason for suspending judgment about the pros and cons of social media; but in the end, I will land on the side of the Platonist. Before that, however, we would do well to focus for a while on attention itself. Until now, I have been suggesting—as the Platonist does—that distraction is bad, and focus on one's goals and plans is good. But is it always so? Or indeed, to what extent should we be focused and to what extent should we allow for distractions?

The (Virtue and) Vices of Attention

At its core, attention is about attributing relevance. In each moment of conscious experience, out of the myriad features of our perceptual and mental landscapes, only a handful of them seem to be so relevant as to enter our awareness. This way our cognitive systems help us cope with the world: by reducing the baffling richness and complexity of experience into a few chunks that limited minds like ours are able to process. We automatically disregard most of the features of our environment as irrelevant (and then they just fade into the background of experience), but some of them acquire the special glow of relevance: they appear more or less clearly in our worlds.

Relevance can be determined by us (endogenously) or by our environment (exogenously). This is why, roughly speaking, we can talk about two main kinds of attention: attentional control is our capacity to focus on the task we are performing by attributing relevance to the features that are related to said task, while also ignoring or inhibiting unrelated features; this is how the endogenous process of attention works: when we set a goal for ourselves, our minds surround the task-relevant features with the glow of relevance. Such endogenous control of attention is necessary whenever we try to perform a task that is difficult enough to require some cognitive processing, or sufficiently extended in time to require sustained focus—like the children in the marshmallow experiment, who need attentional control in order to avoid the temptation of eating the marshmallow.

On the other hand, attentional capture occurs when some external event grabs our attention, so to speak, without our permission. If someone loudly pronounces our name, we often cannot but notice, even when we are deeply concentrated on some task. Sudden loud noises (e.g., a baby crying on a plane or a fire alarm), bright blinking lights, and fast approaching objects are good at capturing our attention, regardless of what we are doing or whether we would rather ignore them. These are exogenous processes of attention: they originate from outside of us, and our paying attention to them results from an involuntary, automatic reaction. These reactions make evolutionary sense, since they are our way of noticing unforeseen features of the environment that may require immediate responses.

So, the objects of attention can be established endogenously or exogenously; and different people have different tendencies: some people's attention is more easily captured than others, and some people can more easily keep their goals in mind and avoid diversions from the original plan.

Now, what would be the best distribution between endogenous and exogenous attention? I want to push forward the idea that excesses in either direction are problematic so that we can call such excesses "vices of attention" and that, in an Aristotelian vein, the virtuous distribution of attention lies in a middle point between those extremes.

Vices of Attention

Imagine someone whose attentional contents are determined solely from outside: she cannot maintain a unified attentional pattern, but rather is constantly attracted by features in her perceptual array that invite her to respond to them: she sees a chair and feels invited to sit on it; she sees a sweater and is invited to put it on. In fact, something like this seems to occur to people with a neurological condition called "utilization behavior," which is roughly characterized as the appropriate usage of objects in inappropriate situations.[6] Utilization behavior patients seem to have lost sensitivity to broad aspects of their practical situation and respond immediately to any of the environment's affordances (i.e., the possibilities for action afforded by the currently present objects, agents, or dispositions of both). They also seem affectively insensitive to the inappropriateness of their actions. Thus, a patient with utilization behavior may continuously switch a light on and off; if upon seeing a comb she may start combing her hair with it, regardless of who owns it; if she is in a bedroom she may undress and go to bed, even if she is just visiting someone else's house; she may drink from a cup of coffee that is on the desk, although it belongs to her doctor. And after doing any of these things, the patient seems unaffected by the awkwardness caused by her behavior. A patient may even give reasoned accounts for what she does: she may acknowledge the cup belongs to the physician and explain that she drank from it because she was thirsty.

In a sense, utilization behaviors are correct: the patients use the objects skillfully, as they should be used (e.g., they do not drop the coffee cup, but appropriately drink from it, and then place it back on the table). Still, although these behaviors display some kind of control, we would hesitate call them "actions"—they are mere reactions to the environment's affordances, exogenously driven automatic responses that fail to display the unity and coherence characteristic of human actions. Utilization behavior makes patients change the focus of their attention from one aspect of the environment to another without any regard for their own plans or motivations. In fact, arguably, the main feature of utilization behavior is that patients have lost their ability to form and carry out plans and motivations of their own.

If we picture a spectrum of attention, with completely exogenous attention at one extreme and entirely endogenous attention at the other, an extreme form of utilization behavior would lie at the exogenous extreme: an attention whose focus is always determined by capture. This is evidently problematic, since it makes it impossible for the agent to perform actions or follow through with plans requiring any complexity, and this ultimately leads to a thorough inability to shape our identity. This is, thus, an erroneous way to attribute relevance, and thus constitutes a vice of attention, a sort of hyperdistraction.

At the other extreme, we find that concentration may lead to a sort of blindness. In a popular experiment, researchers asked participants to watch a video that shows a basketball team in action and count the number of passes the team made. The movements were fast and hard to keep up with: for many of us, this would require our undivided attention. That is why a large number of participants fail to notice when someone dressed as a gorilla zigzags between the players, steps in the center of the scene, hits his chest with his fists, and walks away.[7] The "invisible gorilla experiment" is the most famous case of inattentional blindness, the phenomenon in which we are so busy performing a cognitively demanding task that we become effectively blind to things that would otherwise capture our attention. This is the flipside of attentional control: when we focus deeply on a task, the rest of our environment fades into the background, even if it includes gorillas hitting their chests in front of us. There are more mundane cases of this: when rushing to a store just before closing time, you may fail to notice a friend of yours waving at you trying to say hello; you may be looking straight in her direction, but she is effectively invisible. Such is the inhibitory power of attentional control.

That is obviously a problem: we often should pay attention to unexpected elements of our context even if they are unrelated to our current task, since failing to do so may constitute errors in our attribution of relevance that could have grave consequences (think about failing to notice the smell of gas in your home because you are so immersed in the latest season of *House of Cards*). Thus, at the other extreme of the spectrum lies the opposite vice of attention, in the form of a hypothetical case of a fully endogenously driven agent, who would then be thoroughly inattentionally blind. This hypothetical, inattentionally blind character is never distracted from her tasks and her attention is never captured exogenously, which would entail dismissing as irrelevant some features of the situation that happen to be relevant. This faulty attentional pattern could thus be called hyperconcentration.

Thus, we have two vices of attention corresponding to the two extremes in the attention spectrum hyperdistraction (a case of thorough utilization behavior, where relevance is always exogenously determined) and hyperconcentration (a case of thorough inattentional blindness, where relevance is always endogenously determined). Given that the two extremes correspond to two vices, it makes sense to think with Aristotle that, in this case, virtue of attention is somewhere in the middle between these two extremes.

Virtuous attention is that of an agent who attends to what is relevant, in the amount that is relevant, and while it is relevant. Her subjective sense of relevance corresponds to real relevance in each given occasion; she keeps her mind on her goals and attends to the things that are relevant to them; but whenever something outside of her task's realm needs to be taken under account, her attention is captured by it, which enables her to find an appropriate response. This is obviously an ideal, and I present it, as well as the aforementioned idealized extremes, as tools for the analysis of the effects of the social digital media on our habits of attention. So, let us return now to that question. In terms of endogenous versus exogenous relevance, are social media bringing us closer to or pulling us further away from the virtuous mean of attention? Before answering this, we should ask: how are we, for the most part average Western human beings, located with respect to it?

Akratic Attention

A large body of evidence suggests that our normal habits of attention deviate from virtuous attention in quite a number of ways, by systematically misattributing relevance. For instance, we tend to see losses as excessively more relevant than gains, and to see immediate pains and pleasures as excessively more relevant than distant pains and pleasures.[8] Moreover, and to the present point, we seem to be more easily distracted than the virtuous agent would be, since average human cognitive and executive capacities are severely limited. It is very hard to keep our attention focused on the same task for long spans of time, especially if this requires filtering out distractors.[9]

This implies that we are rather bad at multitasking. More precisely, we rather suck at it. Some people are better at it than others, granted; but we should rather say that some people *suck less* at it than others. The key problem is that, as it turns out, we cannot process multiple threads of information in parallel, because our core capacity for effortful information processing—called "working memory"—works serially, that is, one bit of information at a time. Since true multitasking would imply processing multiple streams of information through multiple processors but as we have only one working memory, we cannot truly engage in true multitasking. What we can do, instead, is shift between tasks. Task shifting is generally less effective than serially performing one task and then another because each task implies attributing relevance to different things, and so things that are relevant for one task become distractors for the other tasks. So, multitasking (or rather, task shifting) implies a loss of efficiency, because we have to add the costs of task shifting (of redistributing relevance and cancelling the prior distribution of relevance) to the costs of serial processing. People who say that they are good at multitasking may just be bad at noticing how inefficient they become.[10]

So, it is harder for us to keep endogenous control of attention than it is to have it exogenously captured by a diversion, and multitasking increases the likelihood of distraction. This suggests that we are closer to the vices of hyperdistraction than to those of hyperconcentration. In fact, we could say that we tend to suffer from a sort of "akratic attention": like the children who eat the marshmallow before the adult returns, even if we wish to keep our focus on the larger, later reward (a consistent exercise routine, a healthy work-life balance, a committed romantic life), we often cannot help but be distracted by the temptations of the smaller, sooner rewards in front of us. So, our attention is akratic in the sense that we tend to lack the self-control we wish we had. External diversions tend to capture more of our attention than they should, like when we spend too much time on Facebook or end up jumping from one hyperlink to another. We easily procrastinate to avoid performing the most difficult, most attention-demanding tasks. We crave novelty and get all too easily bored, and this often results in an overall pattern of attention that lacks unity that is spread toward many directions and fails to make unifying sense. Of course, there are people who successfully control their attention and achieve their long-term goals without too much effort, there even are people who go to the other extreme and obsessively control the minute aspects of their lives. But, excess of distraction is much more common than excess of rigidity when it comes to attention.

(How) Are Social Media Changing Attention?

If self-control depends crucially on our proper distribution of attention, that is, on our proper attribution of relevance, if the virtues and vices of attention are as presented above, and if we tend to have a rather akratic attention profile, what are the effects of social media on our attentional capacities? Are they changing the way we shape ourselves? And if so, is this change for good or for bad? I move on now to summarize what the available evidence says on this issue, and speculate about the possible effects that social media is likely to have on our attention and self-control in the future.

Two Diverging Attention Profiles

The explosion of social media is still very recent, and science has a lot of catching up to do. For now, we have only a handful of studies that try to establish the relationship between social media, attention, and self-control. Keeping in mind that we are just starting to delve into these issues (and so what follows is largely provisional and should be revised in light of new evidence), this is what we know so far.

Several studies suggest that high levels of social media engagement are associated with lower academic performance, especially in heavy multi-taskers. The more people tend to multitask between using social media and studying, the worse they do at the latter.[11] And the harmful effects of social media seem to go further than that: a recent study found that people were worse at exercising self-control after five minutes of browsing Facebook than after five minutes of browsing CNN.com. In comparison with the CNN group, those in the Facebook group were more likely to eat an unhealthy snack over a healthy one (thus showing they are more likely to succumb to temptation) and tended to persist less in a difficult task (thus revealing they tend to be distracted or give up more easily). Researchers conclude that "the effect of social network use on individuals' abilities to exhibit self-control is concerning, given the increased time people are spending using social networks."[12]

Besides lower academic performance and lower self-control, higher levels of social media use are also related with a lower ability to filter out task-irrelevant stimuli. In other words, people who report spending more time using social media, like Facebook and Twitter, have also been found to do worse at endogenously controlling their attention. More frequent social media users, it seems, are more distracted people—especially if they use social media in multitasking situations, a trend that is increasingly popular, and increasingly demanded by jobs that require immediate reaction to messages and e-mails.[13]

This all looks admittedly grim. But interpretation of these data demand caution: here, as elsewhere, we must be extremely vigilant not to confuse correlation with causation. Given the way these studies were designed, all we can infer from them is correlations and not causal links.[14] Thus, so far we know that high social media usage is associated with lower levels of attention and self-control; but from this association, we cannot infer that social media are causing an erosion of attention and self-control. This is because several different possibilities remain open: it may be that something else (say, lack of sleep or dietary deficiency) is causing both high social media use and low self-control, or it may also be that it is low self-control that causes higher levels of engagement with social media. In fact, many of the researchers suggest that people who spend less of their time on Facebook and the others may do so because they are better at self-regulating and more goal oriented, so that their concern for their performance in school or at work may be controlling their use of social media and their multitasking tendencies by making them better able to focus their attention endogenously. We also do not know whether people are currently more distracted or less self-controlled than before: evidence of a different, harder to obtain kind would be required for that.[15]

So, is social media causing us to be more distracted? We simply do not know. This should give any Platonist pause. That said, what we do know is that people who are more actively engaged in social media also tend to be more easily distracted. In fact—and to put it in less evaluative terms—what researchers have found is that social media use seems to mark a distinction between two divergent profiles of attention, which they call "breadth-biased" and "focused" attentional control.[16] I will refer to this as the distinction between a broader attention and a deeper attention.

Such divergence may be enough for Platonism 2.0 to get off the ground. If social media are linked to a broader attention profile—which is in turn associated to higher levels of multitasking, lower levels of self-control, and higher rates of distraction—then the use of social media is associated with a shift away from an akratic attention and toward a vicious, hyper-distracted attention. Even if social media are not causing this problem, they surely are not helping to solve it. Ultimately, then the evidence supports the view that Web 2.0 multitasking goes hand in hand with lower levels of control over the shape of one's life, with a weaker construction of one's self; so that if they are not the root cause of the problem, they still are far from being a part of the solution.

This Platonist comeback makes sense, but it is arguably not inescapable. For as Plato could not have foreseen the possibilities for self-construction opened up by the technologies of the book, we may be unable to foresee the new paths of self-construction enabled by the new digital media.

New Medium, New Self?

I have portrayed self-control as the ability to shape one's own life by determining which desires and intentions are effectively translated into actions, and thus more globally as the subject's capacity to give a specific contour to her own identity. Self-control is grounded on the capacity to persist in one's plans in the face of obstacles and persevere in the face of temptations; it is sustained by the subject's stubborn will to shape her own self. The view of the self as something that the individual generates, sustains, and nurtures from within, by exerting selective control over her desires and intentions, is at the core of the new Platonist's concern.

Platonism 2.0 is the alarm of a self that sees that its means of self-forging are taken away from under its feet.

Those means were—among others, but crucially—the technologies of the printed book and their widespread use. The dominance of the book as a medium meant that a single person could dig deeper than ever into her own consciousness and expose in meticulous detail what was there to be found. This is what made modernity's novels, philosophical treatises, and scientific monographs possible. The reader was also conceived of as a reflective individual, capable of following the sometimes dense, often long, most of the time linear plot or line of thought exposed in the book. And thus, writer and reader could form a community of reflective individuals capable of reasoned dialogue. The case can, therefore, be made that the printing press strengthened and, to some extent, generated this kind of linear, reflective, thoughtful agency, along with its ideals of self-control and autonomy.[17]

Now, with the drastic change of medium, a correspondingly drastic change of self may well be unavoidable. Electric mass media like television and radio transformed the slower speeds of the printed word, but retained its linearity and unidirectionality. Digital social media represent a more thorough transformation, because they add to the immediacy of electricity their hyperlinked and interactive nature. So now, instead of the slow-paced, monologic, and unidirectional medium of the book, and instead of the unidirectional and linear media like television, we have the massive, immediate, hyperlinked, and interactive media of the Internet. How will those radical changes in medium be reflected back onto the formations of agency and the self? We will have to wait and see.

One thing to look out for is whether the broader profile of attention will enable us to create new kinds of abilities. For although we do suck at multitasking, at the same time multitasking is crucial for our ability to acquire new skills. To see why, picture yourself trying to learn a new musical instrument. When you first pick it up, the difficulty of performing the most basic tasks is enormous: synchronizing the movements of fingers and arms and legs with the rhythms of the breath or the focus of the gaze requires our multitasking capacities at their maximum. But with practice, these different behavioral routines get automated and unified into action "chunks" that we are better able to perform with less and less effort as we continue to practice. This is the effect of automation: we unify multiple complex behaviors into single units of synchronized, less effortful action that we can then control intuitively. Practice makes it easier to identify the few really relevant bits of information, and thus liberates attention. That is how we learn how to simultaneously walk and talk, play the guitar and sing, take a Snapchat and hang out, and so on.

Now, it is possible that new, broader forms of attention enable the emergence of chunked actions that were impossible for traditional, narrower attention profiles. As possible examples, one may think of new kinds of musicians who now use the computer to simultaneously compose, mix, perform, and promote—processes which were until recently quite distinct and for which separate specialists were needed. This may open up new, vast creative spaces that were previously unthinkable, new kinds of activities, skills, and trades. If computers and smartphones are understood as general-purpose extensions of working memory and the Internet as a general-purpose extension of our senses (both bodily and social), then the possibility exists for novel and unforeseen forms of chunked actions that externalize the cognitive costs onto the computers and the Web, while merging multiple threads of diverse behavioral routines into coherent, basic actions that we have until now been unable to perform. Along these lines, the transformative broadening of attention generated by new social media would enable us (or rather, future generations) to engage in multimodal, collaborative, multidisciplinary, geographically discontinuous actions that are still unimaginable today, much as the individualizing, deepening actions made possible by the book and the press were unimaginable for Plato.

If this is what novel actions will look like in the future, what may the future self be like? This will have to be a less endogenously determined self, based more on its exogenous responsiveness to multiple threads of online stimuli than on its capacities for planning and maintaining focus, more on new ways of quickly coordinating with others (on the reactions it gets from others in the social media) than on the old capacities for slowly constructing a long-term individuality. An emergence of this new kind of self should lead us to reassessing the virtues and vices of attention. The new virtuous middle, corresponding to the new virtuous self, may move away from the hyperconcentrated and closer to the hyperdistracted. Only that now we should probably not call the attentional capture by features extraneous to one's current task "distraction," but rather "responsiveness," "alertness," or "embeddedness." A broader attention has the ability to be more attuned to what is relevant out there, beyond my own individual plans and goals. The new, online self would thus redefine how we should understand what is truly relevant, making it more about being attuned to the flows of information than about staying focused on my current mission.

This all sounds very neat. But it is probably wrong, for it loses sight of one key feature of skill acquisition: it is slow, it is hard, it is effortful, and it requires persistence. This persistence is what makes some people become great guitar players while others never learn more than a few chords. And at the highest levels, the greatest persistence is what distinguishes world-class performers from great performers. There has recently been a fascinating debate about the nature of skill and expertise, in which anti-intellectualists (led by Hubert Dreyfus) defended that as an agent progressed in skill she needed less and less executive control of attention, until when she finally reached the level of expert she could do without it entirely, merely following intuition and feel. This has turned out to be very controversial, and the most recent, most exhaustive empirical evidence seems to go against it, and lean in support of a more intellectualist view, according to which attentional control is required even at the highest levels of expert performance. As you become more skilled and advance to the higher levels of an art, a sport, a craft, and more, things also become more difficult and the possible diversions increase enormously. In order for experts to perform at their best, they need to stay focused. And this implies great endogenous control of attention.[18]

If the intellectualists are right (as I argue elsewhere that they are),[19] then Platonism 2.0 still has the upper hand regarding the effects of social media on agency and the construction of the self. Acquiring a skill in more distracting environments requires even more endogenous control, because agents need control over their attention to thread the multiple behavioral components into a meaningful, unified action. Without this great level of endogenous attentional control, what is most likely is that, in the short run, agents end up lost in their multitasking, having forgotten mid-performance what it was they were trying to do in the first place; and that, in the long run, agents will end up unable to create new, flourishing skills and virtuous selves, rather generating incoherent, haphazard characters and identities. Even multitaskers need executive attentional control to reach the heights of skill and expertise. Therefore, even new generations will probably need self-control to generate new kinds of selves.

Concluding Remarks: A Dream Left Unfulfilled

Here is a final question: if the emergence of a new dominant medium implies that something proper to the previous one will necessarily be lost, what is it we are likely to lose? And how fundamental and crucial will that loss be?

Much like the previous questions, for the most part we will have to wait and see. But this much seems certain: the Enlightenment dream, in which each individual will be able to abandon his tutelage and think for himself, thus forming a community of autonomous minds able to engage in careful, reasoned debate about any issue, no matter how thorny, is likely to become increasingly distant as we move to the new world of multitasking and distraction. For, arguably, the rise of immediate, massive, interactive media has coincided with the rise of an emotivism and intuition in the public sphere that tends to bury dispassionate reflection and reasoned debate under a mountain of gut feelings and intense reactions, all quickly expressed, replicated and made viral through Facebook and Twitter.

This, again, is sufficient ground for a Platonist worry, particularly considering that the most pressing problems of the contemporary world—like climate change and global economic inequality—tend to be very hard to understand, require much deep reflection, and not be easily communicated in 140 characters. Some kinds of content are better suited for microexpression via tweets and for comprehension by short attention spans, and they again often coincide with reactionary, emotional messages that people can understand intuitively. So, what we may ultimately be losing, if we lose the dream of the Enlightenment individual, is the very possibility of a functional, reflective democracy that is capable of discussing a topic without being distracted away from the topic by a tweetworthy, rhetorical sleight of hand.

One may think then that digital technology, being an "extension of man," may help us better understand these problems and more effectively come up with reasoned consensus about them.[20] But the problem is that technology, as far as social media are concerned, seems to be pulling in the other direction, favoring attentional breadth over attentional depth, brief spouts of impulse over careful and dispassionate reflection. Instead of building new scaffolds for our attentional control, new technology may be removing the previously set-up scaffolds. (This is, of course, partial. There are new Internet-based scaffolds; it just seems that the new diversions are more powerful, but this is a topic for another essay.)

So, will the cognitive extensions of technology lead us toward a renewed Enlightenment? Or will they push us away and into a social formation that is at the same time newer (in its massive synchronicity) and more archaic (in its focus on collective intuition rather than individual reflection)?

For now, the jury is still out. But I would not get my hopes up.

Notes

1. Some of the initial findings can be found in W. Mischel and E. Ebbesen (1970) and W. Mischel, E. Ebbesen, and A. Raskoff Zeis (1972). (The experiment's setting is somewhat simplified here for presentation purposes.) Follow-up studies are reported in Y. Shoda, W. Mischel, and P. K. Peake (1990) and T. R. Schlam, N. Wilson, Y. Shoda, W. Mischel, and O. Ayduk (2013), among others. See also D. T. de Ridder, G. Lensvelt-Mulders, C. Finkenaur, F. M. Stok, and R. F. Baumeister (2012).

2. In this short characterization, I am skipping over a number of discussions concerning the philosophy of agency, self-control, the will, and their mutual relationships. For discussion, see Frankfurt (1971); Heath and Anderson (2010); Paglieri (2012).

3. The story is narrated in *Phaedrus* 274C–275B (tr. by B. Jowett).

4. Carr (2011).

5. The response to Platonism from a group of anthropologists who have recently studied the uses of social media around the world goes along those lines.

6. Pandey and Sarma (2015). The condition was initially reported by L'Hermitte (1983), and is linked with bilateral damage to cortical and subcortical locations in the medial premotor system. For discussion of the syndrome and its relevance to agency and control, see Baddeley (2007, Ch. 17); Rietveld (2012).

7. Simons and Chabris (1999).

8. These phenomena are called "loss aversion" and "hyperbolic temporal discounting" in the literature. For the former, see Tversky and Kahneman (1981); and for the latter, Ainslie (2001).

9. See E. Ophir, C. Nass, and A. D. Wagner (2009).

10. See A. C. Karpinski, P. A. Kirschner, I. Ozer, A. Mellott, and P. Ochwo (2013) for a review of multitasking in relation to social media use.

11. S. M. Rouis, M. Limayem, and E. Salehi-Sangari (2011); Karpinski et al. (2013).

12. Wilcox and Stephen (2013). It is worth noting that only those who reported strong social ties with most of their Facebook contacts presented lower levels of self-control. The effect was not found in the weak ties group.

13. Ophir et al. (2009); Rouis et al. (2011); Alloway and Alloway (2011, 2012); Karpinski et al. (2013); Wilcox and Stephen (2013).

14. On why obtaining causal evidence in this case is particularly difficult, see Karpinski et al. (2013: 10).

15. A recent statistic quickly became viral, stating that our attention span had diminished in recent years. Researchers from Microsoft Canada (2015) say that the average human attention span (the average time we spend on a single task before getting distracted) was 12 seconds in 2008, but went down to 8.25 seconds in 2013. The attention span of a goldfish is 9 seconds, so now we have become more easily distracted than goldfish. This, like any scientific-sounding

factoid found online, should be taken with some skepticism. Microsoft cites "Statistic Brain" as its source for the human–goldfish attention span comparison. This turns out to be a website in which the data are indeed reported. But none of their sources seem to check. So, the whole thing turns out to be based on a made-up rumor.

16. See Ophir et al. (2009) and Lin (2009). Many of the previously cited researchers make an analogous distinction.

17. This is an argument made by Carr (2010), which he himself traces back to McLuhan (1964).

18. The classical anti-intellectualist position was developed by H. Dreyfus as a reading of phenomenologist Merleau-Ponty (see e.g., Dreyfus [2002]; Dreyfus and Kelly [2007]). Recent anti-intellectualists (like Brownstein [2014]) have had to face a resurgence of a refined kind of intellectualism (e.g., Fridland [2014]; Montero [Forthcoming] for in-depth discussion).

19. Bermúdez (Forthcoming).

20. The diagnostic of the problem of speed in the public sphere and the possibility that technology, among other environmental scaffolds, may extend our cognitive systems, is put forward in Heath (2014).

CHAPTER FIVE

Does Social Media Interfere with the Capacity to Make Reasoned Arguments?

Chris Beeman

Does social media interfere with the capacity to make reasoned arguments? I began to ask this question a few years ago when I noticed that my students were writing progressively less well-reasoned essays. The information required to make an argument was there, but the argument itself was not made. These essays had the feel not so much of being rushed, such that reasoned thought had not been given time to properly steep, although this may also have been a factor, but that the ability for clear argumentation had actually been lost, so that, when it was missing, it was not noticed by the writers themselves. This chapter addresses the following questions: How might the predominant locus of knowledge acquisition amongst young adults and the foundation for social media—the Web—be leading to different kinds of argument making and concepts around what constitutes an argument amongst these "knowledge consumers"? How might this contribute to a different sort of identity? Might my students' style of writing not be only a failure to reason? Might their work represent a new way of argumentation, whose time has come? And further, might linear argumentation no longer be necessary, except for certain, limited tasks?

Introduction

I am concerned with what appears to me to be a rapidly dwindling capacity on the part of some university students to produce good arguments. By *good* here, I mean arguments that are valid in form and that are based on reliable sources of information. I think the two aspects are probably linked—a person might be more susceptible to trusting unreliable information if they do not know how to make valid arguments—but this paper focuses on the quality and kind of arguments themselves. The first question that I wish to address in this paper is: how might the predominant source of information amongst young adults and the foundation for social media—the Web—lead to different understandings of what it means to construct an argument?

The principles and technological structure of the World Wide Web (hereafter, the Web) make possible social media. Social media are described as "Internet-based applications that build on the ideological and technological foundations of Web 2.0 and that allow the creation and exchange of user-generated content."[1] Thus, the technological interconnection of the Internet is combined with the open-source information space of the Web to provide a powerful new locus for person-to-person creation and sharing of information in the form of social media. Some would say that social media are a natural consequence of what the Web makes possible. At root, social media are reliant on the Web as the basis upon which their particular functions are made possible. Thus, in this chapter, the influence of the Web as a whole on reasoned thought is considered because it undergirds social media.

Understandings of Reason

Imagine you are instructing a university course and that you receive an essay from one of your students. It is a short essay; the assignment only calls for a few pages. The essay is about, say, poverty as a factor affecting education for First Nations students. One paragraph describes how poverty in general has implications for learning; another describes historical reasons for First Nations' current poverty; another refers to early treaties covering this geographic region and their provision for education; another, to Métis culture; another contains a quotation from a novel; another, a quotation from an interview with a First Nations representative; another, a quotation from a representative from the provincial government. The ideas from the different paragraphs are not connected by a clear argumentative thread. Then, a conclusion is presented.

Essays that take roughly the form above—that is, a mass of possibly relevant information with no apparent argument leading to a stated conclusion—have been submitted to me more frequently in recent years in my role as a professor. I need hardly point out that not all essays are like this, but in my world, an increasing number are. And here is the main point: the conclusion that my students reach in their papers is not one that can be derived from any discernable linear argument in the essay, although the component parts could be ordered and connected in ways that *could* produce a strong argument. What is presented is a cluster of thoughts that are related, a pastiche of sometimes interesting, interrelated ideas. The feeling I get in reading each paragraph is one of scrolling down a Web-based search page to the next promising prospect and finding out what it has to say. This is, in part, what leads me to question whether a Web-based kind of information gathering has led to new expectations or understandings of what constitutes an argument. In the essays in question, it appears that little or no thought has been given to presenting the line of argument nor, perhaps more significantly, is there any indication that the writers felt the need for it to be included as part of the essay.

At the same time as there being a lack of explicit argument, it appears that the writers believe that they are making at least *some kind* of argument. It is almost as if the argument is so patently clear, based on the information selected to be presented, it is not necessary to overdo things by actually taking overt steps to direct a certain conclusion. I am reminded of the fastidious deliberation that a 20-something sometimes displays before making that actual phone call—the making of which to me seems so innocuous—rather than sending the usual text. In interpreting such deliberation, and the sentiment that appears to be attached to the making of explicit arguments, I am left with the impression that both are regarded as something like ill-mannered intrusions, and that therefore discretion ought always to be the better part of, say, communication.

In summary, there appears to me to be at least two things occurring in the example of the essay that I gave above. The first is that an explicit argument has not been made. By an explicit argument, I mean that pre-suppositions and propositions are clearly stated, probably or likely thought-moves or steps are taken, and a conclusion is reached. The second is that the writer appears to *think* that an argument has been made. Leaving aside, for the time being, the possibility that what appears to be an increasing frequency of these kinds of papers arriving in my inbox may itself be the sloppy result of the time demands of Web-based learning, it seems to me to be worth looking into how thought and thinkers may be changing.

The second point—that the writer appears to think an argument has been made—is perhaps the more interesting of the two, because there exists the possibility that the writers may be simply deluding themselves: there may be no argument of any kind. But, the writers may also feel that there has been *some* kind of argument made, and that I, as the relatively unhip instructor, lack the context or conceptual ability that would allow me to make sense of this new kind of what might be called "cluster meaning-making." In other words, there is something to this amassing of information acquired by sifting through the endless piles of possible stuff on the Web that might count as some kind of argumentation.

Ludwig Wittgenstein, in passages relating to language use, invokes family resemblance as opposed to definition as a way to understand word meaning and relationships between ideas. But he also plays with the notion of a sentence, teasing apart its various interpretations, in order to address how what were thought to be clear, reasoned ways of understanding, may change. In Section 108 of *Philosophical Investigations*, he writes:

> We see that what we call "sentence" and "language" has not the formal unity that I imagined, but is the family of structures more or less related to one another.—But what becomes of logic now? Its rigor seems to be giving way here.—But in that case doesn't logic altogether disappear?—For how can it lose its rigor? Of course not by our bargaining any of its rigor out of it.—The *preconceived idea* of crystalline purity can only be removed by turning our whole examination round. (One might say: the axis of reference of our examination must be rotated, but about the fixed point of our real need.)[2]

I confess that the later Wittgenstein only makes sense to me as a kind of poetry (I will return to this idea later), and while you may think that this will take me straight back to how I ought to read undergraduate essays, let me pause for a few moments to try to make some sense of what Wittgenstein appears to say. And by "make some sense," of course I mean in a way that can speak to the (unhip) linear, argument-forming part of my mind. Given the context of this passage, Wittgenstein appears to be suggesting that as soon as we question what constitutes a sentence and as soon as this causes us to question the use of language, we are presented with questions about how logic—of the kind I want to find in the passage above but am prevented from doing so—by language itself may operate. Its "crystalline purity" must give way for a new kind of logic (or it is reason?) to replace the old. And to do so, we must "turn the whole examination round," by rotating the reference points of our examination, still paying attention to what our (investigative) needs are. Well, that is a lot clearer!

Perhaps it is clearer to posit that Wittgenstein, by persistently questioning, was encountering and trying to convey the limitations of what language could do. This was in the sense of language *qua* language, certainly, but also, by extension, as a tool for "doing" logic. Or, perhaps it was as a tool for facilitating reasoned thought itself. Is it possible that at the same cultural moment that my students are immersed in social media, language (and what it "does") is not just contracting, but so changing that reasoned thought is also morphing into something quite different?

From a very different research perspective and from two-thirds of a century later (but perhaps not coincidentally from the same university), Iain McGilchrist also has a lot to say about reason. McGilchrist comes at the subject from a pointedly neuroscientific route, and from an examination of how the two hemispheres of the brain enact different *ways of being*[3] in the world. Made possible by recently developed brain imaging techniques, McGilchrist argues for what might almost be called a different "culture" for each hemisphere in *how* thought occurs.

Recent Magnetic Resonance Imaging studies show the brain as being much less discretely segmented in task and much more adaptable than had earlier been thought. Earlier understanding of brain function, based on machine and computer models, saw particular parts of the brain responsible for particular kinds of work. But studies of people with brain injuries show that function can be rerouted or that there are many different pathways to perception and thought. It now appears that activities that were thought to be localized in one area or hemisphere may occur in the opposite hemisphere or throughout the brain. The application of reason is a good example of this. While linear and sequential argumentations are better executed by the left hemisphere, deduction and mathematics are mainly dependent on the right.

With these more complex understandings, Iain McGilchrist dismantles the earlier oversimplified notion of the language and symbol-ready, logical, left brain as opposed to the "creative" right brain, which is present oriented, global in awareness, visual, and emotional, to show that reason—and human identity—lies not in one hemispheric mode or the other, but crucially involves aspects of both. There is a hemispheric divide made necessary, he believes, because of the relatively recent exigencies of mammalian life, which demanded a capacity for two simultaneous modes: one involving more global awareness and one suited to immediate and linear tasks. These were needed to perform two separate but equally essential demands: to maintain vigilance against predation and to do linear, focused tasks such as food gathering, tool making, and eventually having conversations.

So, there is a reason for the regulation of communication between hemispheres, because it would be easy for one to interfere with the function of the other. The corpus callosum, which connects the hemispheres, is designed to both facilitate and to control communication between them. And, here is the key: each hemisphere experiences the world fundamentally differently and we are never in the mode of being of both hemispheres simultaneously. Each lives, as it were, in the same apartment, but remains unaware of the other, because their modes of being are precisely that which tends to preclude perception of the other. They are never in at the same time. But despite this, the dishes occasionally remain unwashed, and this can lead to conflict.[4] In McGilchrist's understanding, there is a kind of power struggle between the hemispheres; in the modern world, the left almost always wins.

McGilchrist suggests that researchers ought to pay more attention to the *how* of brain function, rather than simply what was investigated historically—the *what happens where* approach. The left hemisphere is certainly specialized for symbolic interpretation and the right for breadth of perception and visual imaging, and with these proclivities, ways of problem solving vary. For example, "Here the right hemisphere presents an array of possible solutions, which remain live while alternatives are explored. The left hemisphere, by contrast, takes the single solution that seems best to fit what it already knows and latches onto it."[5]

This takes us right back to Wittgenstein. There have been many attempts, especially in Philosophy, to make sense of these two fundamentally opposed experiences of the world. What Wittgenstein might have been getting at, using the available tools, was that there are discernible moments in which the usual force of reason does not apply. I do not think it is a coincidence that it was in a reexamination of language that, itself a left brain mode of operation, his questions around logic—which the acquisitive left hemisphere would like to claim as its sole purview—that his doubts arise. His term "turning the whole examination round" sounds eerily prophetic in this neuroscience context. I imagine a revolving of hemispheres within the brain, their relative cultural importance simultaneously shifted. And that his work reads best as poetry—meaningful, but not in the way the left hemisphere favors—is perhaps indicative of the kind of challenge he was presenting.

It might be tempting to see the "old style" reason that I appear to be asking from my students as "analog" and the "new style" reason that my students are giving me as "digital," with the former corresponding to left hemisphere pre-Web thinking and the latter corresponding to right hemisphere Web-oriented thinking. But this would simply be wrong. If anything,

I think the "new style" of reason is so left brain mode oriented that it has lost track of the need to both be present and conscious of steps in thought while they occur, and to make these steps known to those with whom one wishes to communicate. One of the really critical problems I foresee, if Web-based reasoning of the cluster meaning-making kind persists, is a reduced ability to understand that another person, who knows the same information from the same sites as you do, might reach a completely different conclusion. Perhaps, following McGilchrist and Wittgenstein, the global sensing of a new kind of "evidentiary force" might be something in us sensing that here lies another way, without quite knowing which way to actually go.

So, when they write essays for me, of the kind I mention above, my students think they have told me something that constitutes an argument. And I do get a rough idea of where the points they list appear to be leading. But I do not understand an argument—at least, not in the way that I am used to calling understanding. Is this simply saying that, were there more time for my student to "frame" thought, their thoughts could be joined and arranged in the form of linear argument? Or is it that they do not see the point of this work? Their evidence has been, after all, presented to me just as it was found. Surely, I must reach the conclusion they did?

Taking this notion further, and following up from the earlier hunch about explicitly and self-consciously made arguments as a kind of intellectual intrusiveness that parallels the social intrusiveness of a phone call, it is almost as if, in the midst of such a mound of information, it would be somehow biasing my own relationship to the knowledge, for my students to both present the information and to make an argument that brings it together. Surely, this is pushing the idea of bias too far. But even if it is, if this does occur, it suggests that something different is happening for these students in the way they formulate arguments; something like that the information, if presented in the way they encountered it, is self-evident. There is no place and no purpose in linking thoughts, through reason, to arrive at a conclusion.

Or perhaps it is more than this. Is it that my students are not even digesting knowledge (and encountering thought) in the same way as I do? Perhaps, they have never had the experience of the kind of understanding that is entailed in steps in thought, each of which is reasonable, leading to some place they did not at first think they would get to. Perhaps, what works for them is what works for search engines: the limitlessly large numbers of people encountering—or not—an idea or person or image and liking or unliking them, thus leading to what has been called a democracy of thought.

But, here is the problem: thinking clearly is not like this, and I think neither is democracy. Perhaps, they both can never be. What some of my students are doing is a massing of thoughts with the hope that, in the sheer numbers of related ideas, an argument, like the invisible hand of the economy, will emerge. I have had a similar feeling, I think, while navigating fast-moving water on a river. I imagine myself trying to navigate the fast-flowing water of a difficult little set of rapids. In this circumstance, there is a kind of line of reason that corresponds with an intended course through the rapids. But this is almost never the same as the course that one actually follows, because the exact force of this day's water motion on this shape of hull with this day's paddler's energy always changes what is possible. So, my intended course also changes with what the flow of water and the day brings.

Thus, in this favorable reading, my students might be, as it were, reserving judgment to allow the flow of the water to guide argumentative direction. And perhaps, according to McGilchrist's interpretation of hemispheric style of thought, this willingness holds many possible problem solutions in mind at once, which is more right-brained in manner. But, here is the difference: the paddling course I initially intended (however, it may differ from the actual one) has something to do with me making it through the rapids: the very intendedness of direction gives me the possibility of understanding things about the river that I would not do, if I simply left myself to the mercy of the current or sat on the bank. In other words, to give the analogy away, an argument that is intended, even if it fails, may permit certain kinds of recognizing, understanding, and even perceiving that are distinctly different from the simple gathering of information. This suggests the value of employing reasoned argument in the process of learning.

In this less "environment-influenced" kind of thought that I think may favor the formulation of arguments, thinking clearly is an ordered assembly, with each piece meaning something particular in relation to what preceded. It is not simply a grouping of interesting ideas, but only related ideas, with a background hope for meaning-making. Thinking clearly also involves patience, a deliberation that does not demand instant understanding. It tries out various ideas in relation to others and tests them, honestly, for whether they "ring true."

It is still possible for me to speak with my students and to reason about reason, as it were: to show the difference between "good" arguments and those that are not. But the influence of social media on the formation of users is one of the key ideas emerging in this essay. That some of my students appear to not be able to express themselves in terms of linear argumentation suggest that they are being constructed by the tools they use, to becoming different kinds of people.

The students who write this way appear not to be conscious of their listeners as needing an explanation that takes account of the line of argument itself. Philosophers are used to other philosophers telling them what the form of the argument will be, as I did at the beginning of this paper. This presupposes an imaginative capacity for what the other, hearing the argument for the first time, might be going through. But some of my students do not seem to have this. The recent electoral groundswell to be rid of Canada's last prime minister Steven Harper was reasonable in its direction, but perhaps concerning in its form. The question it raises is, when everyone appears to agree, how do you know when you are "getting it right?" There seems to be little doubt as to the inevitability of the position their audience will reach, when the mass of information that my students have accumulated is presented. There are many international examples of social media's capacity to influence political direction. What is perhaps more concerning is the effect of "crowd-think" at a global scale.

If there is uncertainty about getting it right, then there must also be concern about getting it wrong. And this prompts the question, in groundswell decision-making: how would participants know if it is "wrong?" I can imagine a kind of tit-for-tat exchanging of information between disputants, each of which is unwilling to invoke reason for fear of making some postmodern blunder. Surely reason itself and the moves it considers justified would be suspect in this scenario. The trouble is that, without a model, and without perhaps a sensation of what it feels like to be certain for reasoned reasons, there is no way to tell if a good ("well-reasoned") conclusion has been reached. Perhaps, in practice nowadays, it is just the person with the most screen stamina who will win arguments by amassing the most information.

In the arena of large-scale decision making, if we come to rely on this "massing together" at the right instant, might this have an inhibitory effect on other ways of making decisions? For example, I am wondering, given Harper's abysmal record on the preservation of democratic institutions, why such a groundswell did not happen earlier. Might the "tipping point" not then yet have been reached? If this is the case, and if we rely too heavily on things like a "tipping point," which might actually get it right but too late, and if we do not have other quicker and more overt means of deciding—like intentionally using reasoned argument—perhaps this will mean that we come to lack a significant culture-wide tool for making decisions, and that democracy itself is altered.

Identity

The next question I wish to address is how might this contribute to a different sort of identity? Maxine Greene's notion of freedom, in her *Dialectic of Freedom*, is not one of "choosing between"—in the way, say, I might expect to make choices between sites on a Web-based search of a topic. I choose this site, and this one, and this one, and these tend to send me in these directions (especially under the influence of algorithms motivated by my preferences). I tend to "feel" a certain way about a subject. And I am "drawn" to a certain conclusion. (I need hardly point out the possibilities for misuse of search engine designers here.)

But for Greene, freedom is inextricably linked to the capacity to effect change in the world.[6] And the capacity to effect change must be linked to both the capacity to perceive information in it clearly—or at least to be able to take account of one's bias, as it intersects with what the world appears to be presenting—and to the capacity to evaluate and link what is encountered to other information and ideas. Without these capacities, the Web is endlessly varied, endlessly depressing, and just plain endless. My concern is not simply that a less *reasoning* person is being generated through interaction with the Web; it is that a less free one is being generated, all the while being lulled into believing that its "freedom" (of the choosing between kind) is beyond limitless.

There are several other issues of identity that may come into play. One is imaginative capacity, mentioned earlier. It is a different thing to reason than to gather. In reasoning, one needs to be able to imagine what a person would think who does not accept one's position, then to construct an argument that could convince someone who holds this different position. Related to this is generative capacity. In a reasoned argument, one creates something that was not there before, which is the argument itself, rather than just gathering and amassing related ideas. And, as above, there is also the capacity for freedom. Freedom consists in acting in the world; the other kind of freedom—the capacity to simply choose between options—may be characterized as a more sophisticated kind of consuming.

The Demise of Reason or a New Kind of Argument?

Faced with understanding my students' essays, there is another possibility here: that my students' work might represent a new way of argumentation whose time has come. In this view, my approach is simply outdated. The argument against my position might go that yes, as the capacity for directed reason naturally atrophies, there may be the odd glitch when it comes to determining reasonable conclusions, but there are other benefits. To begin, there is something to be said for the way in which large amounts of information can give a certain impression of things, which linear thought alone cannot. It may be that we will simply come to mass facts together and throw it at our intellectual opponents. Or perhaps there will be fewer and fewer opponents, as we agree (facing our screens) on the apparent undeniability of what is concluded.

But I want to contest this on two counts. The first is simply that reason is really good for some things, like choosing between two (summarized) positions. The second goes back to the notion of existential freedom. I think that the scenario above is not simply misguided; it also represents a loss, because a capacity to act in the world to effect change that is desired by the person is inextricably linked with freedom.

In this vein, I turn again to Ludwig Wittgenstein. In his description of language-games, he looks into games themselves. And here, he looks into all kinds of things that are called games: board games, sports, card games, and so on. But, in presenting them, he finds that there is no element common to all of them. Olympic Games and Ring a Ring o' Roses, for example, are both kinds of games, but have little to do with board games. So, there may be no one common thread that joins all language games. As he writes,

> I am saying that these phenomena have no one thing in common which makes us use the same word for all,—but that they are *related* to one another in many different ways. And it is because of this relationship, or these relationships, that we all them all "language."[7]

Wittgenstein is using language games as a way to get to a deeper idea of the nature of philosophical propositions. He again turns to another analogy—this one of family resemblance. And, while this is not the purpose for which he invokes this idea, I want it to be ours. I want to propose that what Wittgenstein says about family resemblance, as a way to understand language games, and thus propositional ideas, might also be a way to understand another way in which ideas could come together to make a kind of argument.

Say that the parts of my student's essay that I mentioned long ago, and that I faulted, based on the lack of continuity and step-by-step linking of the central ideas, were actually linked in a different way—that is to say, the way that Wittgenstein wants to consider the similarity of language games based on family resemblance. No one member of a family looks identical to another, but perhaps a baby has a way of making a certain expression or a nose like Aunt Martha's (dang)! Say that each of the themed paragraphs in the example of the essay given at the start of this paper—the implications, in general, of poverty for learning, First Nations treaties, and so on—that each were not stepping stones in an argument whose direction was determined, but rather served as overlapping layers in a kind of, say, mille-feuille or lasagna argument. Each part, each added bit, had something to do with another, but was not quite a "logical" step from the other. But the combination of ingredients, characteristics, or factors would in each case lead inexorably to a conclusion. In this model, the layering of ideas might form a structure, giving a strong "feel" for a conclusion rather than requiring certain definite steps be taken to reach it. This kind of argument, like its Web source, may be web-like in structure.

This may be giving my students too much credit, because I am quite certain that many do not give much thought to creating logical arguments; but then again, it may not. In much the same way that many have never owned a home telephone, they may simply choose to skip over the teaching or technology, if linear reason could be called that; they may not need it. But what troubles me is that last emphatic adjective of two paragraphs ago: *inexorably*. Perhaps, this is an increasingly rare treat—like a good lasagna—that we may well frequently have to forego.

The succulent satisfaction of a well-realized dish may embody the increasing rarity of the problem solving that goes into cooking well. The hash that comes from a spontaneous mixing of ingredients—perhaps with some consideration given to friendly flavors, but with no real end in mind—might be a more common object of consumption. There is nothing wrong with a mishmash of flavors for everyday eating, but it is a pleasure to find a kind of culinary solution rather than simply a happenstance discovery, from time to time.

And this brings me to my last question: might linear argumentation no longer be needed, except for certain, limited tasks? I do not think so. The image I am coming to rests on the idea of changing gears, with gears being the various ways in which we reason. It might work, in addressing certain cases or problems, to use my students' agglomerative approach. One can imagine a case in which, over a relatively short period of time, a wide, societal movement edges toward a certain position. In this case, it is useful to feel the sway of others, despite the obvious dangers. The Web, as expressed through all of its systems, is almost unlimited in its capacity to inform and include multiple perspectives in this way. But being informed of others' movement can also be dangerous, unless the tool of reason is employed to check and assess it. And it is this tool that is being sharpened in the writing of papers in which an explicit argument is both made and is known to be made. In fact, I think that the capacity of my students to write papers that follow a line of argument—with flexibility, surprises, questions, curiosities, all included in this—reflects not just a particular ability, but also state of mind that is central to the capacity of groups and persons to make decisions. This state of mind includes imaginative and generative capacity, and the capacity to exercise existential freedom.

Notes

1. Kaplan, Andreas M., and Michael Haenlein. "Users of the World, Unite! The Challenges and Opportunities of Social Media." *Business Horizons* 53, no. 1 (2010): 61.

2. Wittgenstein, Ludwig. *Philosophical Investigations.* Translated by G. E. M. Anscombe (Oxford: Basil Blackwell, 1958).

3. McGilchrist, Iain. *The Master and His Emissary* (New Haven and London: Yale University Press, 2012). Coincidentally—I mean this literally—at about the same moment in time, I used precisely the same phrasing to describe ontos of First Nations elders with whom I was doing research. The name appears as part of the title of my doctoral dissertation: *Another Way of Knowing and Being.*

4. The analogy is my own; I think McGilchrist would accept it.

5. McGilchrist, Iain. *Master and Emissary.* p. 41.

6. Greene, Maxine. *Dialectic of Freedom* (New York: Teachers' College Press, 1988).

7. Wittgenstein, Ludwig. *Investigations.* Section 65.

CHAPTER SIX

Exclusive Spaces

Alex Leitch

Exclusivity is a form of privacy used to establish value. To be exclusive is to promise hidden secrets: a challenge. Challenges, correctly constructed, offer agency. To be cool, a message or service must be illegible enough to incite an exploration, a sense of legitimate risk while minimizing the sense of threat. The sense of discovery offered by services like YikYak or Snapchat allows more agency, and thus more loyalty, than other, more public services. This chapter amplifies on the point made in the Introduction, "The Role of Habit," and by the Pew Research Center people about how young texters and social-media posters learn to doctor their communications with exaggeration, selective omission, and other means to enhance their images.

Introduction

In 2010, no one in Canada had any money for building new experiences. The 2008 American recession had just landed, removing raw capital from play just as the tech economy was starting to look north. At the time, I had finished art school and graduated into the bad news, only to realize with some friends that the bad news was unlikely to stop for people in our position. If we wanted to do something cool, we were going to have to build it ourselves, and we were going to have to make other people believe it was worth doing. We were going to have to build it ourselves, sell it ourselves, and make sure it kept running ourselves, with no access to venture capital. The seed funds we had came solely from various members' wages.

If you are going to try to build something secret, something exclusive, it takes more than capital alone. Alongside capital is the need for a good story, which is normally accessible via straightforward expenditure: pay enough and you can get a brand at any one of a number of houses. This will not work for building sustainable prestige, because it represents a one-time expenditure delivered by parties outside the group—the group will grow in its own direction regardless of what has been designed for it, and may not be interested in what was designed by an outside party. Therefore, building a successful space that works on no money is more difficult than spending money: the space needs to generate an aura internally to retain value. It needs a trick, it needs prestige, or it needs to be secret.

Secrets are more valuable now that lives are lived online and in public. For young people especially, privacy is at a premium, and can never be assumed. Facebook has blown the concept of privacy as a default away, with constantly shifting privacy settings that all but guarantee context collapse—the experience of information being presented to an unintended audience—in its users. Things are being disrupted all the time, a word that can be interpreted as "removed from the social contract" or "removed from pre-existing legal and social frames of understanding." This disruption is destabilizing, and prompts people to find new ways to construct in-groups.

At the same time, being isolated and in public all the time drives a demand for privacy and community. When everyone can have everything, scarcity itself becomes valuable, and when everyone lives online, a memorable, loyalty-inspiring experience is probably going to take place in the physical world.

Facebook, Snapchat, and Exclusivity

Into this arena of social disruption comes social media, the way people talk to each other in public—that is, in a legible way—in the 21st century. Too much exposure on social leads to context collapse, but too little leaves one isolated from one's peers. As social media frameworks come of age, they also come to "belong" to specific demographics because of this possibility for context collapse. Context collapse is the consequence of the presentation of information to an unintended audience, when that presentation destroys a carefully constructed public image. Avoiding context collapse is the central promise of privacy.

Privacy within a social network is constructed differently for young people than for adults.[1] In particular, Facebook and networks designed for adults—networks designed for maximum commercial reach—frequently subject their users to a choice between context collapse and intensive hand management of various social connections, which includes manual construction of those networks. This extra labor is intensive, and represents a transfer of value from the user to the network in the form of legibility. For teenagers, who have a lot to hide from their parents, this labor is essential.

This extra labor is built out of hours of time, which are of implicit value to their users, if not explicit value. By constructing personas that are visible and road-tested in public, and engaging in "social stenography," young people are able to test out a personality before displaying it in real space.[2] Social stenography is the use of messaging such that meaning is hidden from unintended audiences even when it is unavoidable that such messaging will be seen by an audience as outside its intended context. Within Marwick and Boyd's research are several examples of extreme models young people have taken to restrict public perceptions of themselves: a young woman deactivating her account during office hours only to reactivate it for chat functions in the evenings, for example.

Facebook, famous for privacy violations, has sealed itself to a demographic that is comfortable with a broad audience: adults who have already formed their sense of self, and their public image. This limits the possibilities for surveilled young adults to participate in a Facebook-style media network without an extra layer of labor on top, composed of the "social stenography" Boyd describes as a practice to hide oneself from context collapse.

This is where Snapchat's value—if value is constructed as the capital represented by a reduction in labor—appears: Snapchat is intentionally illegible. If one does not know a user's username in advance, the service provides few discovery tools. It has been built to hide information from unintended audiences in exactly the reverse of Facebook's super-public system. Privacy from authority intervention is an explicit part of the design, and those authorities include parents. This is desirable to youth, who want privacy from the surveillance of their parents, and what youth want youth make cool.[3]

In a service like Snapchat, the surveillance of context-collapsing local relations is assumed as explicit. Snapchat has been designed to at least appear to have messages delete automatically after a small window of time, and in so doing, has directly integrated a value system mainly designed to appeal to people who are subject to direct surveillance rather than the indirect surveillance of massive data sets. This direct appeal necessarily restricts the appeal Snapchat can have to a demographic that has a broader participation with other demographics. The affordances of Snapchat are that "social stenography" is an acceptable cost of doing business, and that in return, content shared on Snapchat will represent an "authentic" self.[4]

This argument: Facebook, as the big public versus Snapchat as the private circle, is the heart of how to construct an exclusive space or service. Snapchat's privacy feels simultaneously safe and risky: you can send whatever naked selfies you like with the promise that they will delete themselves after nine seconds, whereas making the wrong joke on Facebook might see one facing down consequences years after the fact. That the photos may or may not be on the server after the fact is inconsequential, as the design affordance of the software provides a sense of security to the user.

Making Hackerspaces

The design affordances of social networks help drive demand for surveillance-free spaces with solid community in the real world. Thanks to a quirk of timing, in 2010, my peers were primarily hackers who had emigrated because they did not like the direction of America's warrantless digital search policies. They were specifically concerned with the normalization of surveillance—not just the information shared on Facebook, but also involuntary data collection. When they came to Canada, these security professionals brought knowledge of hackerspaces—a type of professional club dedicated to breaking into computer systems thought to be secure. Hackerspaces need to be surveillance-free in order to let hackers work through computer problems, as even necessary research into computing system flaws—flaws that can lead to bank information dumps—can be illegal. Even apparently complete software is full of near-fatal flaws, however, and hackers know it.

In this, hackers have something in common with artists: both groups have a professional interest in illusion and prestige. In the case of computer security specialists, the illusion is that anything ever shared on a network can be made private. In the arts, we have a different specialty: generating prestige fields similar to Walter Benjamin's concept of "aura" around physical objects and performances.[5] A prestige field is a field people fight to get into which pays poorly, exchanging material reward with the regard of one's peers in the form of a sense of "cool" or similar.

Examples include almost any work in the arts or nonprofits. Prestige fields come up in magic, where they literally represent the final sleight-of-hand illusion, but they also back black-tie fundraisers, or any work in an art gallery. A prestige field is what dictates that a piece of contemporary art—maybe an inverted ladder or a bicycle wheel on a stool—is of material value. The value is an illusion. By their very nature, prestige fields reward people as much for the appearance of who they are as for the paperwork filed or tickets sold. Indeed, the tickets sell primarily because of the prestige: people like to be fooled. This same sense of value, what a design might be worth, is at the heart of the computer science debate about consumer hardware and software, whether an Apple system is truly worth the 30 percent margin increase over similar hardware to be found elsewhere.

Apple, at time of writing, is worth approximately US$775 billion dollars. Prestige, done correctly, is a big market—but at the same time, it is a limited one, which tends to power laws.[6] Power laws are a mathematical rule that governs what are popularly known as "hockey stick" charts—they represent a field where one entity wins very big and everyone else in the field almost not at all.

Together, my peers and I wanted to build something that would have a prestige field, and leverage that field into a place where we could encourage members to explore what they thought of as possible within the bounds of work, in order to transfer power from existing systems to a fresh population.

One of the most important elements of creating Site 3, and hackerspaces more generally, is that these are spaces specifically to conduct work, and work that is about prestige. To generate a prestige field is a similar task to building an effective magic trick or a coherent online persona: it requires tight regulation of what is revealed and what is on display. This is part of the broader discipline of experience design. There are many reasons to put together a workshop, but the access to tools supplied by a workshop environment is not enough to ensure that workshop members can actually build something cool or see upward career mobility. Instead, members must set a high bar for what constitutes a full team membership, and clear pathways with consistent achievement models for what will permit acceptance within a ritualized space oriented toward labor.

Computer security specialists are early members of the gig economy. Often freelance, they are part of an increasing population of workers who operate in isolation, and their trade is specifically in disruption—not just the disruption touted by app manufacturers, although this type of systems thinking is useful for that, but also the disruption of communications tools and social norms. Being persistently outside the norm can be lonely, and my peers described hackerspaces as places researchers could go to normalize their trade. This type of secret-locked club has a longer history in earlier periods of labor disruption and economic migration.[7]

In his 1959 *Primitive Rebels*, Eric Hobsbawm writes about how at the turn of the 19th century, ritual labor organizations helped overcome loneliness and disconnection in recently urbanized populations of laborers. These organizations relied on secret rituals and costuming, hidden lodges, and heavy use of symbolism to generate secular cults. There are clear parallels between the secular labor cults and today's hidden makerspaces and exclusive clubs generated by newly disrupted populations working in technology, who form the primary audience for co-working facilities.

To make something seem cool and other from the norm, labor cults relied on pseudoreligious ritual. In today's largely secular society, the role of religious ritual can be imitated or replaced by an appropriately magical piece of technology. The technology has to form a point of focus and community involvement, much like how an altarpiece might appear to grow a church around it, though the church itself is the true focus of the community. The use of technology to supplant a holy book gives people something to talk about that has tangible results. For best effect, the chosen tool or technology should be learned and something that has to be consciously maintained. The learning appeals to the people who want to use the technology to produce something, and will use the tool or technology to do so, where the maintenance appeals to people who would like to learn about the tool itself. Both groups can then learn "secret" knowledge, and develop an interdependence on one another, which leads to community. It is best if the technology is not personally risky to use, because that will limit the audience who can be involved with it.

In the case of early makerspaces, a laser cutter provided a suitably "future" feeling piece of technology that is also clean enough to avoid the class issues surrounding more practical piece of manufacturing technology, such as a mill and lathe, which carry with them actual rather than perceived risk. A laser cutter may seem dangerous, and frequently has warnings on the case, but does not carry with it the very real risk of more serious personal harm present in accidents with classic industrial equipment. Laser cutters seem cool because they make something happen in real space, apparently cleanly and without much real personal threat. A laser cutter represents an acceptable personal risk that, because of its lack of apparent grime, feels future-y—the same way drones feel more like the future than gas-powered model airplanes. The future, in 2010, was still clean enough for people who did not work with their hands to have a look in at it, and that is the key to exclusivity.

Trade-oriented pseudoreligious ritual has long legs, which stretch back to the last industrial revolution. The concept of these labor cults is the topic of Eric Hobsbawm's "Primitive Rebels," which provides detail on how secret membership keys and especially ritual help to stratify and make coherent diverse groups in periods of "disruption," which are better characterized as social upheaval. Symbolic rituals are popular in technologist circles, as are semiprivate labor cults. There are several examples of these useful to showing how technology values exclusivity. The original and best is Burning Man, home of the idea that one must participate to be fully present, or the Further Future Festival—which is Burning Man without the work, and consequently without the loyalty, or the House of Latitude, a secret immersive game in San Francisco brought low by the leader not quite understanding that community is as community does.[8] The labor is important, however: the labor is the initiation ritual. In computer science initiation rituals, as in art, the achievement is not the prize: the prize is more work, and the possibility of participating in the creation of works larger than those capitals alone can account for.

Make It Risky But Not Too Risky

Capital alone is not enough to achieve a truly solid sense of prestige within an exclusive space. Alongside capital is the need for a good story, which is accessible via straightforward expenditure: pay enough and you can get a brand at any one of a number of houses. Building a successful space that works on no money is more difficult than either of these, because the work must be good, but above that, it must have an aura to retain value.

In order to generate a real sense of affection for space, it is not enough to convince an audience to spend money. Capital is by its nature mobile, and it is well established that people care more for things that they have a hand in creating, often overvaluing those objects relative to the production of others and the assigned market value of such a production.[9] This effect—the "IKEA" effect—means that people will love what they work on disproportionately to that which is given to them. In order to create a functioning community, therefore, with a strong fellow feeling, it is important that individuals within that community feel a sense of agency and accomplishment over community productions.

This is what makes productions like makerspaces different than coworking facilities, or any facility that has an interaction primarily based on a commercial exchange: the initiation ritual leads members to being able to work together, and the experience of working together on something over

which every member of the group has some agency leads to a dispropor-
tionate sense of belonging, far more than could be established by any normal office or business experience. The more work a community member
puts in, the more they are likely to feel something is "theirs"—and this
applies to digital identities as strongly as it applies to disposable Swedish
furniture.

Making something cool, and generating a sense of personal involvement, then requires some sleight of hand: a thing must seem risky and
difficult to interpret, in order to present a challenge, but must in reality be
attainable and have a low barrier to entry.

City Construction Alleys

Assuming that an infrastructure of money and volunteers is in place to
assemble a clubhouse at all, the best place to put a secret in a major city is
down an alley in a high-foot-traffic area with good transit connections.
This is particularly true in Toronto, Canada, a heavily gentrified urban
center based around laneway construction in blocks. A laneway is a narrow street—just wide enough for a car or carriage—primarily faced with
garage entrances or small sheds. It could also be an alley, here regarded as
the space between buildings.

Alternate possibilities include innocuous doors opened by electronic
locks, as used by the House of Latitude in San Francisco or The Temper-
ance Society in Toronto, but the architectural construction of limited
space is itself important to risk-taking behavior. Rather than seeming
super-visible, engagement with space—and digital media—is best executed by presenting information in a constrained way. In digital media,
this is executed by Facebook's relatively small apparent reach, as contrasted with its broad actual reach. Sharing settings are notoriously difficult to manage, which is a sleight of hand that strips privacy from users
and necessitates an enormous amount of extra work to prevent context
collapse. This is an example of an unapparent risk that is in fact major. In
order to build trust with a community, it is more important that a risk
seem large and in fact be small.

Laneways in Toronto are not particularly dangerous. Toronto has many
laneways, having been built out of single-family dwellings and carriage
houses, and these alleyways are well maintained. They are also home to
Toronto's thriving street art scene. Exploring laneways and alleys in the
city will lead to the discovery of some amazing murals—and in a pecu-
liarly Canadian twist, some of these are socially sanctioned. There is an
entire wall reserved for graffiti just off the main shopping strip, which

means that Torontonians who pride themselves on being cool have already been socialized to walk down alleys and through laneways. The most vibrant Toronto district, Kensington Market, is composed almost entirely of alleys, secret bars, and hidden things. In Toronto, exploring very safe yet theoretically dangerous areas is part of city life. It would be hard not to walk down a lane in Toronto at least once. There are Jane's Walks, named for Jane Jacobs, and neighborhood explorations, and deputations to city council for laneway names.

In the case of a makerspace down an alley, the prestige is here: laneways and alleys in Toronto are very safe, but Toronto is subject to American media consciousness. Alleys are constructed as dangerous in the American media consciousness: Batman's parents get shot in an alley; children are warned not to take shortcuts on the way home. The gap between the mediated ideal of what is happening and the reality of what is happening allows some magic to slip through. People can be expected to feel brave for engaging with the city on their own terms, even as Torontonians live down alleys and have kilometers of garages facing lanes. By asking people to engage with curiosity about their space, there is the possibility to generate a special experience, something hidden but available, with reasonable confidence that an audience will pursue the experience.

The theoretically dangerous is a major part of exclusivity: it is where the magic happens. The illusion here is that someone is taking a big risk, or a risk that is really past their personal boundary for such things—this represents a bid of emotional energy—but which is in practice unlikely to result in a bad end. Things should have, for example, the image of physical harm, or the possibility of same, but that possibility should be remote in truth—the result of consciously poor choices. Such risks are easily found in places that have this construction of cult-like magic: "Keep Burning Man potentially fatal" as a motto, for example, but most injuries at Burning Man are from stepping on rebar or sunstroke, not from the many vividly threatening flame effects. The risk keeps people awake, but the relative safety makes it okay to explore, to push that boundary.

A magic trick, then: select a group who have little enough at stake to be willing to explore, while being just scary enough to encourage people to have to overcome some fear and to feel invested in the exploration. Rewarding an expenditure unpredictably is a sure way to encourage people to spend more,[10] which is what one needs in a space designed to run on no capital. The effort has to come from somewhere.

The experience design of a bid and reward in a contained space is well described in Natasha Schüll's book on machine gambling, *Addiction by Design*. Schüll describes how casinos go out of their way to produce alleys of machines with tight corners that permit privacy from other players, in order to encourage gamblers to feel safe to play—to make a bet. In addition, casinos go out of their way to hide the way out—to confuse and distract from the passage of time. This is considered a "dark pattern" in site design, a system for manipulating people. In the case of a clubhouse, the comfort is that your secret cannot be too far removed from the main drag, at least to start with, and if you would like the site to appeal to women, it is important that the way out is obvious. In Site 3, we were fortunate enough to find a site quite close to a major intersection and a subway stop. This meant that not only could people take a simple risk to get in, but that the way back to transit was always clear.

This balance of risk is a contemporary form of the psychogeographic game, the *dérive*. The *dérive* is an unplanned journey through an urban landscape undertaken with the intent to be subconsciously directed by one's surrounding architecture.[11] The *dérive* is normally intended to be a kind of meditation, but by providing an actual hidden treasure in reward for exploring, the workshop is able to select for an audience willing and able to take a risk, while always providing an easy way out. The way out being accessible is the difference between building an addiction machine and a space where the audience can consent to participation, while believing themselves to be engaging in a risk-taking behavior.

Initiation Rituals

This pseudo-risk then becomes the first step in what might be seen as an initiation ritual into a type of secret society. The link between a makerspace and a labor cult from the turn of the 19th century may not seem immediately apparent, but both are based in problems around labor and belonging, disruption and loneliness. Many people who work in computer security or the arts are used to an environment where there is not a lot of confidence in the stability of the general economic order. Popular culture is now almost entirely oriented to what used to be referred to as "nerd culture"—comic books, video games, forms of media, and entertainment that are engaging but lack conventional cultural cachet. The shame around being primarily interested in popular culture remains, as does the need to prove one's membership as an "authentic" geek.

Computer security, like the arts, is a prestige discipline. Membership in computer security is entirely composed of careers in finding out or obscuring secrets, and controlling the flow of information: even the social networks are set around initiation rituals that verge on hazing. Enforced drinking, a performative language of military action, conferences that are must be at but impossible to attend, and general machismo is the norm in hacking as a profession. This is not so far off from the arts, where intelligence in producing a prestige field is held as a type of public smarts in opposition to conventional popularity.

Classically, nerd membership—coveted, difficult-to-attain knowledge in the arts or the sciences—is held in opposition to popular status. This form of performance, to be publicly smart rather than popular, leaves both arts and nerd culture open to cliquishness and a need to prove belonging above and beyond that which can be established more classically by, say, joining a softball team. The cliquishness of earned knowledge is an exclusivity model that, conveniently and famously, does not cost money. The usual ask is instead time: time spent developing skill so that something difficult becomes something straightforward. The skill must then be performed so that membership is held to members of the in-group.

Labor Cults and Secret Societies in Disrupted Social Periods

Initiation rituals for secret societies are tied to the labor economy of their time. Perhaps, some of the best-documented secret societies are recorded by Eric Hobsbawm in his *Primitive Rebels*.[12] While discussing ritual brotherhood groups linked to social change, Hobsbwam points out the popularity of intensive training for ritual acceptance within an in-group, even one with a name that might seem silly today. Group names like "The Onion" are featured alongside the "Society of Venerable Souls in Purgatory." Hobsbawm points out that even as the straightforward utility of this training faded over time, it remained in play in decomposed forms,[13] only fading when the rituals themselves decayed from a lack of utility. Hobsbawm has a great warning for the nonparticipatory members of various maker movements, observing that the ultimate decline in the usefulness of ritual brotherhoods came as they began to enforce classism, rather than breaking it down.[14]

Labor organizations in this earlier format were founded in part to help offset the pain of being isolated in a disrupted community. A ritual brotherhood in the context of the 1800s helped to offset the loneliness of newly urbanized members of the laboring classes, separated by a new environment and a new way of doing business. It is easy to see why a similar set of ritual groups would be popular in a period characterized by "disruption" to self, home, and the projection of community. This "third space" theory is behind the brand design of Starbuck's coffee shop—and yet, Starbucks is anything but exclusive. It is instead sharply middle class and designed to be the same everywhere, to the extent that their coffee machines have been redesigned to hide the baristas producing beverages. People still need somewhere to go, and a way to perform belonging to their peers.

A primarily "active" third space—a workshop or a makerspace—is distinct from a religious space where one is passively reflective.[15] This activity means that participation in a labor sect cannot be a purely reflective endeavor; instead, the most exclusive memberships are reserved for the people who are actively trying to promote a type of change, and then perform the labor that generates that change. Historically, this flavor of social change has been labor organization—the unionization of groups in tandem with forming types of religion, such as the Labour Church, which Hobsbawm notes as a rare occurrence. He then provides examples of Methodist cases of labor organization, which is interesting in Toronto specifically, a city once known as "The Methodist Rome."[16]

Toronto, specifically, seems to have been well organized to be the host of a number of makerspaces along this line. The architecture of places matters. As a city built between Scottish Presbyterians and Irish Methodists, the city has a strong orientation to working hard and maybe not playing at all. Toronto is well known as a historically dull and work-oriented place—its nickname was Toronto the Good until the late 1990s. The stereotype of a Torontonian as a buttoned-down suit dedicated to their day job is popular enough to be a running joke in Canadian films such as *Bon Cop, Bad Cop*.[17] The image of Toronto has shifted only recently, as influx of new immigration starting in the 1990s hit a tipping point and began to change the social fabric of the city. The architecture of an ideal life is place specific and affects what people can aspire to within that space. In winter-heavy Toronto, there is an aspiration to a good working environment, which—pure speculation—may have made Toronto the ideal candidate for third spaces organized around work itself.

Makerspaces and hackerspaces are facilities designed for cross-pollination within groups who are working as a reward for having done well at other forms of work. Toronto is also an education center, with four major universities and a culture of walkability in the downtown core preserved by the efforts of Jane Jacobs herself. This history is important, since it preserved laneways, alleys, and the ability to explore on foot, which is a way of putting your physical self at risk, rather than risking something by car—that is, inside a suit of armor. This theory backs the ur-makerspace, MIT Building 20, The Media Lab. Building 20 was built to ensure many disciplines bumped into one another in physical space,[18] and underlines one of the social theme only made bigger by Facebook: you have to be in the room where it happens. It is more important, not less, to be in the room where it happens when there is no material reason to be there, because the immaterial reasons, the serendipity, the illusion, and the prestige: they're the whole trick.

Conclusion

That you must be in the room where it happens is a point more applicable now, with our massively expanded public lives, than it has been at any point in recent history. It is easy to mistake reading something on the Internet in the wrong context as being present, but real organization is the result of feeling a membership and belonging to a space or a group of people. A privacy-oriented social network, illegible to parents and gamified to promote interaction with friends, is a good step to generating exclusive space elsewhere. A partially legible space, such as is available in private chat channels on services such as Slack, is equally good. The best, though, is a physical room. With infrastructure now restricted more and more to the most privileged, the perceived value of being in an exclusive room cannot be overstated.

Making an exclusive space is a matter of balancing architecture of place with the architecture of the society around it. "Nerd" culture, the culture that surrounds the technology industry, of long hours and living to work, is uniquely susceptible to labor cult structures last seen at the end of the 19th century. In labor cults, ritual is used not just to enforce an in-group, but also to achieve social goals. In the 21st century, these goals may seem as straightforward as a good party, but they are in fact about personal agency in a time when things seem too big to control, and personal success seems dependent on a perfect performance of a public brand.

Such communities are most straightforward to produce within cities that have a walkable internal structure, because of the discoverability of a space that promotes in-person exploration. A hazing ritual can be as straightforward as a difficulty in finding the location to attend, but involves some element of personal risk to achieve membership in the in-group and tends to reward hands-on labor—characterized as a do-ocracy or "participation" culture—over money. This shift is in large part because financial capitalism within the tech economy has made money alone less worthwhile than an expression of involvement that requires a time expenditure.

Exclusive, member-driven spaces are an excellent networking device and a historically good system for social organization. In an era characterized by mass surveillance and public legibility, such spaces provide a safe zone for exploration both of self and of creative possibilities that require a trusted in-group. Exclusivity is a magic trick, but then, so is capital.

The gap between perception and reality is sometimes called the prestige, and it is the core of all good magic tricks. Penn, of Penn and Teller, says that the best way to generate a prestige is to simply work harder than anyone would ever believe you did, and to build a prestigious space that generates its own right field without major capital represents at least that much labor. It is a matter of balance and finding the gap between perception and reality, then living there.

Notes

1. Marwick, A.E., and Boyd, D., "I Tweet Honestly, I Tweet Passionately: Twitter Users, Context Collapse, and the Imagined Audience." *New Media Society* 20, no. 10 (July 7, 2010): 1–20.

2. Boyd, D., *It's Complicated: The Social Lives of Networked Teens* (New Haven, CT: Yale University Press, 2014).

3. Gladwell, M., *The Coolhunt*, 1997. Retrieved May 05, 2016, from http://gladwell.com/the-coolhunt/.

4. Boyd, D., *It's Complicated: The Social Lives of Networked Teens* (New Haven, CT: Yale University Press, 2014).

5. Benjamin, Walter, *Illuminations: Essays and Reflections*. Ed. Hannah Arendt. Trans. Harry Zohn (New York: Schocken Books, 1968).

6. Maly, T., *What We Talk about When We Talk about Making*, September 7, 2014. Retrieved from http://quietbabylon.com/2014/what-we-talk-about-when-we-talk-about-what-we-talk-about-when-we-talk-about-making/.

7. Turner, F., *From Counterculture to Cyberculture: Stewart Brand, the Whole Earth Network, and the Rise of Digital Utopianism* (Chicago: University Of Chicago Press, 2010).

8. Laurenson, L., *My Year in San Francisco's $2 Million Secret Society Startup*, March 7, 2016. Retrieved May 05, 2016, from http://motherboard.vice.com/read/my-year-in-san-franciscos-2-million-secret-society-startup.

9. Mochon, D., Norton, M.I., and Ariely, D., "Bolstering and Restoring Feelings of Competence via the IKEA Effect." *International Journal of Research in Marketing* 29, no. 4 (2012): 363–369.

10. Skinner, B.F., *Science and Human Behavior* (New York, NY: Simon and Schuster, 1965).

11. Debord, Guy, "Theory of the *Dérive* (1958)." *Bureau of Public Secrets* 8 (2012).

12. Hobsbawm, E.J., *Primitive Rebels* (Manchester: Manchester University Press, 1959).

13. Ibid., 157.

14. Ibid., 168.

15. Ibid.

16. Houston, C. J. and Smyth, W. J., *The Sash Canada Wore: A Historical Geography of the Orange Order in Canada* (Toronto: University of Toronto Press, 1980).

17. Canuel, E. (Director), *Bon Cop Bad Cop* [Motion picture on DVD] (Canada: Alliance Atlantis Vivafilm, 2006).

18. Risser, Rita, "The Beauty of Building 20," *Architectural Theory Review* 14, no. 1 (2009): 19–31.

CHAPTER SEVEN

Social Media and Communicative Unlearning: Learning to Forget in Communicating

Paul Fairfield

Digital media and electronic technology are becoming less tools than a way of life of thinking, appearing, and preferring. The growing preference for electronic over in-person communication ought to worry observers for reasons that bear primarily on what such communication omits, including the realm of nonverbal expression, nuance, and embodiment. As the preference for e-communication increases, what decreases is not only communicative competence, but also the place in human experience for the unconventional, imaginative, intangible, unpredictable, indirect, incalculable, and non-preordained. The forms of social and cognitive unlearning that accompany the digital age demand our attention.

In the early to middle decades of the last century, it was not uncommon for philosophers, particularly those working in the tradition of existential phenomenology, to write about technology in a way that today seems oddly out of date. Thinkers like Martin Heidegger, Gabriel Marcel, Karl Jaspers, and some others had become profoundly worried about modern technology, in a time when the general public was regarding it with an enthusiasm that was virtually unqualified. Even the atom bomb did nothing to slow the phenomenon that was making its way through the Western world and that continues to pass over us. The worry of such thinkers has essentially been forgotten and replaced with the view that all technology is good technology, provided only that it be new and not obviously less efficient than what preceded it. Philosophers, by and large, have stopped worrying about it in anything like the way of only a couple of generations ago, when Heidegger was noting that we had moved into an age of the "world picture" and of "science-technology."[1] Today, readers (if there are any) of a text like Marcel's *Man against Mass Society* would likely smile at the author's misgivings about radio—the amusing naivety, we might think, of a postwar writer who may have sensed that the world was beginning to pass him by.[2] What, one wonders, would such thinkers make of Facebook, Twitter, YouTube, or the technologies that are destined soon to replace them? If they would not join the chorus, we now think, it is because they would be out of step with the times and, in all likelihood, old. Philosophy has moved on, as has the general culture, and worrying about social media or technology more generally is only so much hand-wringing after the horse has left the barn.

Is there anything that is genuinely concerning, or even philosophically interesting, about social media? Does the topic not put one in mind of certain other contemporary social phenomena—the various facets of popular culture, for instance—which a philosopher or social scientist might deign to speak to as a break from more serious concerns, but with some trepidation? The most common view appears to be that there is nothing there that warrants philosophical comment. To see that this view is an error, we must look deeper than the question of "what the kids are doing," which we in our sensible and sober youth did not, to what they are not (perhaps no longer) doing, what habits they are and are not forming, how their experience is being structured, and how they themselves are being constituted, behind their back as it were. Digital media and electronic technology today are becoming less the tools they are still described as being than something like a way of life, of thinking, appearing, and preferring. The growing preference for electronic over in-person communication in particular ought to concern us for reasons that bear in part on what such communication omits, including the whole realm of nonverbal expression, nuance, and embodiment. As the preference for e-communication increases, what decreases is not only communicative competence, but also the place in human experience for the unconventional, unpredictable, unplanned, imaginative, intangible, indirect, incalculable, and non-preordained. The forms of social and cognitive unlearning that accompany the digital age demand our attention.

When an educationalist and university dean writes that a necessary condition of professors gaining credibility in their students' eyes today is that they be technologically savvy, we have cause for concern. José Antonio Bowen writes: "When you do try to demonstrate that your discipline is relevant, your inability to answer your cell phone has already convinced them that you cannot possibly have anything important to teach them. If you do not have both LinkedIn and Facebook profiles, if you do not tweet or blog . . ., if you do not routinely use iTunes or YouTube, if you do not know how to use GPS, or if you do not share photos on Flickr, Snapfish, or Picasa, then you have an immediate credibility problem with your students." More than this, he argues, educational content itself is best delivered online in the form of podcasts, YouTube videos, Wikipedia, computer games, and social media such as Facebook and Twitter. This is the world that students now inhabit, and if educators expect to reach them, we need to reach them where they live. Students "have been learning from games their entire lives," he continues, "and increasingly they want school to be just as engaging." Bowen further notes that "Students no longer want to come to office hours," therefore communication between professors and students must be electronic and fast.[3]

The author of these words is not alone. Indeed, there is a burgeoning literature on the educational implications of the new technologies, and the prevailing attitude in it is an optimism that borders on triumphalism. While what is happening is surely explainable in part as a merely generational difference (parents, let us not forget, worried about rock and roll too), it is not only youth who share this optimism but many of their educators and educationalists, corporate entities and governments, and a growing proportion of the generations that grew up before such technologies existed. On the other side of this phenomenon are cultural and educational conservatives who look wistfully to a time when almost all communication was face to face, young people knew the canon, listened to classical music, and likely went to church. Nonmembers of the first group are quickly taken for members of the second, but a closer look reveals that there is room for a third way here, one that does not so much split the difference between boosters of social media and related technologies on one side and conservatives on the other, but that asks some critical questions about what is happening to us.

The questions I wish to pursue here begin with a specific matter: what explains the growing preference for electronic over in-person communication, between professors and students, for example? This opens onto a

broader question regarding the habits of mind, preferences, and competences that are learned and unlearned when technologies of the order of
which we are speaking cease being tools and become something better
described as aspects of a way of life, of relating, and of thinking. Human
beings throughout history have been enamored with their technologies as
they have with other artifactual achievements. The pattern is not uni-
form, of course, and many prominent exceptions can be found, but the
larger trend has been toward an optimism that newer technologies as a
rule make human life easier and more efficient. Who in the ancient world
could doubt that the wheel, the ship, the watermill, or the aqueduct enormously benefitted their way of life without any significant downside? The
technologies of which we are speaking are of a different order. They serve
existing purposes while simultaneously creating new ones, and in a way
that largely escapes our notice. The needs (better spoken of as preferences) to connect with friends on Facebook, acquire the latest smartphone, computer game, or "app" are creating changes to our way of life
that call for thinking, in light not only of the expenditure in time and
money that acquiring and using such things involve, but of the larger system of ends, experiences, and habits to which they give rise.

Let us begin with the example of professor-student interaction, although
many other examples would serve the purpose. "Students," as the above-
quoted educationalist points out, "no longer want to come to office hours,"
and instead opt for either e-mail, course websites, or social media. Professors still hold office hours, of course, but they are more likely to spend the
time answering e-mail or text messages from students than talking to
them face to face. The explanation most often offered is that showing up
in a professor's office is an inefficient use of students' time. If students in
the past visited professors in their offices, it was only out of necessity.
They lacked the technology and so were forced to trudge across campus
on foot, perhaps in inclement weather, at an inconvenient hour, only to
stand in line or risk that the professor did not show up. The student might
also have a problem with shyness or anxiety. It is a story of travail and
hardship but with a happy ending, for in time technology made it possible to solve all these problems and get the student's questions answered
quickly without leaving the comfort of their residence room. This story is
mostly nonsense, of course, but the important point bears upon the needs
or preferences that are in play here.

The educational needs of university students have not changed much
since, let us say, the 1980s, when e-mail and the kind of social media we are
discussing did not exist. The telephone did, of course, but it was infrequently

relied on as phoning a professor seemed presumptuous and students seemed well capable of showing up for office hours when they required something from the professor outside of class time. No one, to the best of my recollection, was complaining. Students needed to attend classes, understand the subject matter, write papers, prepare for exams, and so on, as they do today, yet somehow they did it without social media or even (most of us) personal computers. It is not their needs that have changed but their preferences. An example is speed. Before e-mail, students with questions needed answers in some reasonable period of time, and sometimes quickly. If they could not wait till the next class, or if classes had ended and an exam was looming, they managed to show up in the professor's office or telephone him or her there. Today this will not do. It is imperative that the e-mail or text message be sent and the wait had better be short, or such increasingly is the expectation. The technology does not serve a preexisting need; it creates one. The need for speed which Marcel was remarking upon in the above-noted text—he was speaking of cars—is now ubiquitous. Everything must be fast, not just the machines but all our resources, including people. Why everything and everyone needs to be quite so fast is a question seldom asked. It just does. If I must wait a full day for a reply to my message, is there no way to make profitable use of the time? If I never drive my car above a certain speed, Marcel wondered, how much faster does it need to go?

Much in this is silly, but one point that is not concerns the same technological imperative that existentialists and some other social commentators were remarking upon decades ago, which is that modern technology not only shapes our preferences, but also makes demands of us which go largely unnoticed, beginning with the demand to be used and relied upon as an end in itself. As we multiply the machines, we multiply the demands and experience ourselves as part of the apparatus. We create a way of life that is organized around tools that do not serve preexisting needs so much as manufacture new ones and in a way that can hold us captive. The Black-Berry slave, video gamer, and internet junkie are commonplace phenomena of our times, and not only among the young or naive. Students who believe they have no time for face-to-face communication may be quite sincere, as may those who maintain that they have no time for a social life outside of Facebook. The phenomenon is real and it is growing.

What I wish to focus on, however, is not the technological imperative itself, but what may be happening to us in a somewhat different sense. What is happening to our experience and our thinking as technology of this order becomes a way of life? What is it doing to us? This is the more urgent question, and it is not one that many philosophers are currently asking. We live in what Barry Allen has called an "artifactual ecology," a cultural environment that is composed of artifacts and especially technological ones. As Allen states, "for us, culture is nature."[4] There is a profound difference between the natural environment of early human beings and what we would now regard as a human habitat. If early humans were "one with nature," we are one with our inventions and in particular our machines. We do not merely use them; we are of them, constituted by them, in much the way that we are constituted by our habits rather than merely engage in them. An artifactual, and specifically technological, ecology calls forth particular habits of mind and body, and as the technology changes so do we. What, then, is it that is changing?

It is far too soon, historically speaking, to offer anything like a complete answer to this question; however, the surface phenomena are not difficult to see. For one, we are seeing a decline in reading, most especially book reading, including among university students. This is particularly alarming in disciplines of the humanities which crucially bear upon textual interpretation. "For some people," as Nicholas Carr has recently noted, "the very idea of reading a book has come to seem old-fashioned, maybe even a little silly—like sewing your own shirts or butchering your own meat." Carr goes on to cite a former philosophy student who undoubtedly speaks for a growing number: "'I don't read books. . . . I go to Google, and I can absorb relevant information quickly. . . . Sitting down and going through a book from cover to cover doesn't make sense,' he says. 'It's not a good use of my time, as I can get all the information I need faster through the Web.'"[5] It is not only weaker students who now say this, but many of the stronger ones as well. Getting students to read books—including what have long been called "required readings"—has likely never been as difficult as it is today, and many professors have given up expecting this. Any who doubt it can ask their own students, as I routinely do, how many books they have read in the last year and they will see for themselves. We could also ask how many hours they have spent on Facebook in the last week or playing video games, and we begin to get the picture.

We are also seeing the above-noted and growing preference for e-communication over the in-person variety, not only between professors and students but also between friends, relatives, coworkers, and indeed lovers. There is no need to worry about long-distance relationships anymore. It can all be done over social media—just about all of it, and the "just about" qualification may soon disappear as well. What is lost in all of this? At the level of communication—and there are other levels that we could mention—there are competences that such technologies call forth and others that they do not, and we need to think about what these are.

Penmanship is not, but perhaps this is a minor matter. It has been replaced with typing on small screens and keyboards, often with one's thumbs—not an impressive skill, but again a small matter. Civilization has survived worse. Far more serious is the question of communicative and linguistic competence in a larger sense. Twitter not only does not require any such capacity, but also is intentionally designed to make its exercise difficult. E-mail still allows it, but it is far from the norm, there being no digital equivalent of the old letter-writing ideal or anything remotely resembling it. The ethos is one of efficiency, styleless brevity, bland uniformity, informality, and speed. If one cannot spell or construct a sentence, this is nothing to worry about, since nor can the recipient.

What, it will be asked, is there to be worried about in all of this? Are Facebook and others not merely the Elvis Presley of our times, something new and strange to worry the old folks, which in time we will come to see as harmless and indeed as having some merit? Elvis was no Beethoven, but rock and roll did not put a generation on the road to perdition, and nor will Facebook. Let the kids have their fun, and perhaps they will outgrow it someday. Except that they will not. These media will be replaced, but with more of the same kind. The point that must be kept in mind here is that modern technology has an unstoppable quality, which comes from being a worldview and a way of thinking that increasingly lacks an alternative. Heidegger was correct: this is an age of technology; technology itself is a worldview and a way of appearing rather than a set of gadgets alone, and one the alternatives to which are disappearing. Social media are but one of its symptoms.

One need be neither professor nor author to see that the written word matters and to appreciate something of the role it has played through the history of our species. The spoken word matters no less. Competent use of either requires the cultivation of skills which do not always produce a utilitarian payoff, but without which we are in trouble indeed. What is lost in the proliferation of digital technology is a sizeable part—likely a large majority—of the meaning that interpersonal communication contains. When one reads an e-mail message, for instance, one is reading words alone. The same might be said of books; however, the author of a book can normally be expected to have achieved a level of competence with the language which is not expected from writers of e-mail messages. Words on a screen are not devoid of significance, but to say that one can communicate any and all meanings satisfactorily through this medium is like saying one can parent through Skype or make love over the phone. One can try, but it is not—as should be self-evident, but I fear is not—the genuine article. What is missing is the whole realm of nonverbal expression as well as verbal expression that is richer than the literal and informational. Body language, facial expression, tone of voice, indirect communication, intimation, insinuation, double meaning, suggestibility, allusion, irony, subtlety, nuance, and even humor are lost on the screen. These matters are not so many bits of information, but meanings in a sense that can no more be reduced to words on a screen than a human being can be reduced to bare bones without the intervention of death.

Interpersonal communication happens between human beings who are in every case embodied, and their being so is not unrelated to the question of meaning. We typically know, albeit inchoately, that what we read on a screen is importantly nonidentical with the same words verbalized by a person standing before us. The person, for one thing, has (or is) a body, and more or less everything that they say, think, and are is a manifestation of their embodiment. It was Maurice Merleau-Ponty who taught us to see this. Embodiment, he showed us, is no accidental property, but is fundamental to human expression and to the kind of beings that we are in a larger sense. Our embodiment is not separate and apart from the meaning of what we say but informs our expressions in ways of which we generally have some understanding. If this is difficult to see in the case of purely technical propositions, such as $2 + 2 = 4$, it is not difficult in the case of a large majority of the things we say. We do not leave our bodies on a shelf when we speak or write. The mind itself is not disembodied, nor is anything that it does.

So much of what we do and are is governed by habits that we need to ask which habits of thinking, feeling, acting, and preferring the digital age is fostering. As Plato expressed it in the *Republic*, "But if they [the Guardians] imitate they should from childhood up imitate what is appropriate to them—men, that is, who are brave, sober, pious, free, and all things of that kind—but things unbecoming the free man they should neither do nor be clever at imitating, nor yet any other shameful thing, lest from the imitation they imbibe the reality. Or have you not observed that imitations, if continued from youth far into life, settle down into habits and second nature in the body, the speech, and the thought?"[6] Imitation, repetition, and routinization foster habits that can be remarkably resistant to change and that are often lifelong. Reading books, speaking in grammatical sentences, listening, paying attention, and careful interpretation are habits, and so are their antitheses. Consider what habits of mind are cultivated by reading books for pleasure or interest, quite apart from what they might be about. Habitual readers tend to be, among other things, patient of mind, able to train their attention for a prolonged period of time, skilled at interpretation, and perhaps also imaginative, discerning, and critical. They understand the value of whatever literature they are reading and may be broadly curious. Whole worlds are open to them, and although they will not venture into them all, they are aware of their freedom to enter any they wish. Consider now the serious video gamer. Forget the disaffected teenager in his (always his) bedroom; gamers have come a long way from that stereotype and are both young and not so young, male and female equally, educated and uneducated, employed and unemployed. Video games are not for angry loners anymore—or not only them. Increasingly they are being successfully marketed to women and people with jobs. What is the characteristic mindset of the gamer? The answer is variable, of course, but most often their orientation is toward strategic thinking, winning, solving a problem, completing a task spelled out in advance, overcoming an obstacle, and more than occasionally shooting and killing, albeit in a cause that is invariably just. Many games are nonviolent, suitable for children, or ostensibly educational, yet whether we are speaking of this end of the spectrum or that of mindless action, excitement, and spectacle, particular habits of mind typically come into play. These include distraction, divided attention, impatience, conventionality, and instrumental thinking.

What tends to be left out of the realm of experience that encompasses social media, video games, and related forms of digital technology is any significant place for the genuinely unanticipated, unconventional, imaginative, intangible, indirect, incalculable, and non-preordained. What is called "out-of-box" thinking, the call for which is so often heard today while the reality is seldom seen, is not easily accomplished by minds born and raised on systems of technology that determine parameters, ends, rules, methods, procedures, and that in general preordain the full extent of what is possible for us. What technological systems of the kind we are discussing achieve, in short, is order, or the illusion of it, not inventiveness or anything resembling it. I can imagine that a rat in a maze, if it dreams at all, mostly dreams of a life outside of the maze. The prisoner's dream is always to be free of confinement, and it is a dream that is commonplace in our time. Our technology "enframes," as Heidegger put it, and circumscribes our experience in ways we do not easily see, although we do experience its consequences and frustrations. Increasingly our experience is arranged in advance, preformatted, prescribed, and standardized.

Compare for a moment the characteristic experience of one whose formative years are spent in some significant measure being told to "go outside and play" to one who spends the same quantity of time using social media or otherwise in front of a screen. The former is not given a specific task, told what game to play, whether to play with others or alone, nor are they given much by way of rules and procedures to follow aside from simple matters of common sense and some elementary moral norms if they are playing with others. They will sometimes get themselves into trouble, annoy the neighbors, and endure scrapes, bruises, and injured feelings, and they will also become habituated to being in nature, to open spaces, unregulated activity, creating new games, relating to others, forming friendships, and negotiating their way through experiences that have not been planned, scripted, and arranged for them in advance. They might develop a taste and a capacity for freedom, since this is what their experience habitually elicits and requires of them. The latter group knows little of this as they grow accustomed to running through mazes and getting what they want by doing what they are told. Their sense of freedom is Hobbesian: egoistic, strategic, and utilitarian.

Between the former group and the latter, there are profound experiential differences which soon give rise to differences in thinking. Strategic and, above all, conventional thinking is what the digital age appears to be fostering, the turn of mind that believes that for every experience there is a desired outcome, a problem to be solved, and a strategy for achieving it. This will be a technique that others have discovered. It is a matter of cracking the code, following rules others have put in place, figuring out for oneself what others have already figured out, and so obtaining a reward. Ask a teenager or young adult why they use Facebook. One might as well ask a cow why it eats grass. The "why" question strikes them as unintelligible. One does not question ends. One questions means. The ends are self-evident. The point of a game is to win. The point of a blog or internet posting is to be liked by as many people as possible. The point of education is the degree. The point of the degree is to get a job. The point of running through a maze is to eat the pellet. This is the measure of a good life, and everybody knows this. All ends are measurable, and what cannot be measured does not exist. One deliberates only about means, and our deliberation itself is again Hobbesian. One maximizes utilities by doing what everyone is doing, only doing it more strategically. One thinks "critically" by mastering the rules of rational thought. One acts in accordance with best (meaning standard) practices and established procedures, and if one does not know what these are, then one asks the consultants and experts.

We get a clue to what is lacking in a given society at a given time by listening for their aspirations, and the current aspiration to think "critically" and/or outside the box is comparable to the yearning for freedom that is so often heard in oppressive societies. During the Middle Ages, people at least knew that their thinking was orthodox and conformist. In a digital age, we imagine our experience and thinking to be otherwise, and the supposition is an error. The box has us all and as firmly as ever. Marshall McLuhan's observation remains true: "The personal and social consequences of any medium—that is, of any extension of ourselves—result from the new scale that is introduced into our affairs by each extension of ourselves, or by any new technology." Form and content are not simply one, but the point that he popularized (he did not discover it) is that alterations of the former cause alterations of the latter, and in ways that tend to escape our notice. Technologies and experiential media, in general, "configure the awareness and experience of each one of us," and "technical change alters not only habits of life, but patterns of thought and valuation."[7]

The illusion is that technology is content-neutral: there is nothing that one can communicate face to face that one cannot say, and more efficiently, in a text message. There is nothing that an author can write in a book that cannot be boiled down to a "tweet" or posting; the remainder is excess verbiage. There is nothing to an idea of any kind but information, nothing to an experience of meaning but words or images on a screen. For this reason, any experience, including the richest, can and indeed ought to be had via the screen. Hence, the concertgoer would sooner watch the performance on their hand-held device than actually direct attention to the stage. The experience, to be properly had, must be "captured," like so much property, and is controllable as such, able to be shared and had again and again or whenever the desire strikes. The watchwords of this kind of experience are control, order, structure, strategy, instrumentality, access, and availability.

What we are witnessing, in my estimation, is both the "new scale" to which McLuhan refers and a depreciation of any comportment or habit of mind that technology does not call forth. In a technological order, what passes for thinking are so many forms of calculation that follow the rules without questioning them or questioning much of anything in a genuine sense. Learning in any one direction is accompanied by unlearning in another, and the kind of social and cognitive learning that the digital age calls forth is accompanied by forms of social and cognitive unlearning, which ought to concern us no less, and likely more, than what concerned the philosophers of existence a couple of generations ago. Returning to the question of professor-student interaction, what is, or might be, accomplished in face-to-face conversation that does not happen via social media is conversation itself, where this is understood as more than the simple transfer of information. If the course is in philosophy, let us say, and the topic of the conversation is a philosopher's views on a given topic, then unless the student's questions are highly elementary ("Was Descartes a rationalist?" "Yes, he was"), what is likely to ensue is a discussion involving some measure of creative uptake, critique, spontaneity, and some dialogical back and forth in the way of any conversation that is worth having. The tool that is the online "discussion forum" which accompanies many an online or blended course attempts to mimic this, and the result is counterfeit. Students using this tool do not speak; they post, and the difference is readily apparent. The purpose of the post is to satisfy a course requirement. It is not a dialogical act, if by this we mean the expression of an opinion or a question that invites an interlocutor's response. The author of the post need not even check in to read the responses. Their orientation may be, and likely is in most cases (one never really knows), entirely instrumental rather than conversational, a case of what Jürgen Habermas terms strategic action (aimed at gain) operating under the guise of communicative action (aimed at truth). What can happen with relative ease during in-person conversation, and which is all but impossible in any conversation that is mediated by a screen, is that a student's thinking can advance in a way that approximates learning in more than an informational sense of the word. The student who is struggling to understand a text or to sort out their own critical position on it cannot obtain more than a modicum of help from a professor over e-mail or any of the social media under discussion. This holds even for the near-discussion in which lengthy missives go back and forth in something approaching real time and for an extended period. Even this—which is far from the norm—is disembodied, surface level, and entirely cerebral. Real discussion involves a cultivation of intellectual virtues and is potentially transformative. Digitally mediated discussion is as genuine an article as the sound of music played at low volume over poor quality speakers. It is not alive.

Communicative competence includes a certain facility with the intangible and the incalculable. The art of communication calls forth capacities of listening with an open mind, fashioning ideas, interpreting meanings, appreciating complexity, cultivating a sense of mystery, and various others which tend to resist formalization. There is more to it than any linear advance on the truth or maximizing of preferences. When Marcel questioned the technological value of speed, he contrasted the modern traveler, for whom the aim is nothing more or less than to arrive efficiently at a destination, with "the traveler of the old days, and particularly the pilgrim, for whom the very slowness of progress was linked to a feeling of veneration."[8] Communication, in the usual case, is not an act of religion, and while "veneration" is too strong a word for most of what happens within it, it is impoverished when reduced to so many techniques for the transfer of information. Marcel's worry concerned an impoverishing of experience which, he believed, attends the death of the sacred, and it was a religious worry only in part. We need not share his religious commitments to see that there is something disconcerting indeed in the deflation of meaning which attends the digital age. It is not only what cannot be said through social media that ought to concern us, but also a collective forgetting that there exists any order of meaning that defies reduction to our technological media.

That the phenomenon that has moved over us is or may be an unstoppable force should not deter philosophers and other observers from asking critical questions about its meaning and implications. It is a matter that demands to be thought about, even if few today are thinking about it in the manner that it demands.

Notes

1. Martin Heidegger, "The Question Concerning Technology," W. Lovitt, trans., in *Basic Writings*, ed. David Farrell Krell (New York: HarperCollins, 1993). See also Martin Heidegger, "The Age of the World Picture," W. Lovitt, trans., in *The Question Concerning Technology and Other Essays*, ed. D. F. Krell (New York: Harper Perennial, 1982).

2. Gabriel Marcel, *Man against Mass Society*, G. S. Fraser, trans. (South Bend: St. Augustine's Press, 2008).

3. José Antonio Bowen, *Teaching Naked: How Moving Technology Out of Your College Classroom Will Improve Student Learning* (San Francisco: Jossey-Bass, 2012), 30, 32, 62.

4. Barry Allen, *Knowledge and Civilization* (Boulder, CO: Westview Press, 2004), 219.

5. Nicholas Carr, *The Shallows: What the Internet Is Doing to Our Brains* (New York: W. W. Norton, 2011), 8–9.

6. Plato, *Republic*, 395c3–10, in *The Collected Dialogues of Plato*, ed. Edith Hamilton and Huntington Cairns (Princeton, NJ: Princeton University Press, 1987).

7. Marshall McLuhan and W. Terrence Gordon, eds., *Understanding Media: The Extensions of Man* (Corte Madera: Gingko Press, 2003), 35, 93–94.

8. Marcel, 2008, 63.

CHAPTER EIGHT

Prices Paid for Social Media Use

Lawrie McFarlane

Facebook, Twitter, Instagram, YouTube, Snapchat, and so forth revolve around built-in metrics of attention—Likes, Retweets, Followers, and so on—so when we use these apps, we are playing a very addictive game of vying for attention points. As our scores get higher, our desire for attention points increases. When we value another person's opinion, or want to express that we care about them, we pay them in attention points. We desire more and more quantities attention, while investing less time and energy into the quality of our social lives. My favorite example is the case of Essena O'Neill, an Australian teenager who, from 2013 to 2015, became so good at commanding attention on YouTube and Instagram that she quit university after one year, claiming that social media promised a better future. Then, suddenly in 2015, Essena had a public "meltdown," saying that for years she had been lonely and empty: she claimed she pursued high quantities of attention at the cost of living ethically and having emotionally satisfying relationships. She deleted all her social media accounts, and encouraged others to take a stand with her. Unfortunately for Essena, her exit from social media had the opposite of its intended effect. For a few months, her story became a "trending topic"—it was discussed extensively by social media users and even very high-profile traditional media outlets (e.g., *The New York Times*, *The Guardian*, CNN, the BBC, the CBC).

Her name became a search engine optimization keyword—social media content creators started to use her name in the titles of posts, in order to attract more attention. While some of the traditional media attempted to use Essena's story to start a discussion about the psychological difficulties young people face in the social media age, the topic fizzled out quickly. In the meantime, Essena has become an object of ridicule and disdain in her former social media community, who now refer to her as "Queenie (the scene queen)"—someone who pursues the highest rung of the social ladder but is too immature to use her power effectively. They read her story as one of failure to appreciate the "real" value of being able to command a lot of attention.

In his 1936 movie *Modern Times*, Charlie Chaplin plays an assembly line worker who becomes stupefied by the repetitive tasks he must perform. When the machines grind to a halt one day, he continues desperately trying to maintain the rote behavior his job requires. The mind-numbing effect of routine physical labor has been well documented. What concerns me in the first section of this article is a different form of mental numbing, namely that associated with cellphone use, the Internet, and social media, particularly among young people. I will go on, in the second section, to discuss some of the ways in which digital electronic communications media and devices are intruding into the workplace with unanticipated and often destructive consequences.

A recent U.S. survey found that among teens aged 13 to 17, more than half sent texts to friends every day. In comparison, less than one in three actually met with friends on a regular basis. Moreover, the prevalence of texting is growing rapidly. The average teenager now sends 3,000 texts per month. How do they find time for this staggering output? For one thing, one in five gets out of bed at night to text.

Cellphone use has become nearly ubiquitous. It has been estimated that more people have cellphones worldwide than have indoor toilets. One widely recognized effect of this phenomenon is its destructive impact on civility. It says something about the tendency toward boorishness in our species when restaurants and movie theaters have to post signs telling patrons to turn off their cellphones. Even then, some just cannot comply. An illustration of this compulsion goes as follows: You call someone and she or he tells you, "I can't speak now, I'm in a meeting." Well, fair enough, but what is he or she doing sitting in a meeting with a cellphone turned on? Does it depend on who calls?

However, the behavioral implications of texting and cellphone use I want to examine in this article are more subtle and insidious. Both cellphone calls and texting offer what appears, at first glance, to be a significant advantage over other means of long-distance communication: near instant response times. In the workplace, but also when relaxing, it can be highly beneficial to contact a friend or colleague and receive an immediate reply. No doubt, many an imminent work-related disaster has been averted by a timely "heads-up" from someone in the know.

Yet, there is an unseen price to pay for this rapidity of response times. Actually, there are several prices. The first price we might term desexualization. According to a survey conducted by the Japanese Ministry of Health, Labor, and Welfare, 36 percent of the male population aged 16–19 has "no interest in sex." Japan's Family Planning Association reports that 61 percent of single men have no girlfriends. Among single women, the figure is 49 percent who have no boyfriends. The main explanation given by these desexualized adults is: "I don't know how to start a relationship with a member of the opposite gender." The Family Planning Association calls these men and women "herbivores," for their apparent lack of carnal desire.

One observable consequence of this retreat from procreative adulthood is Japan's declining birth rate. It is generally accepted that a society's minimum viable replacement birth rate is 2.1 children per woman, during the course of her life. However, by 2005, Japan's birth rate had fallen to 1.3. Nor is this in any way a purely Japanese phenomenon. The birth rate in Germany, Spain, and Italy today is 1.4 and in Canada 1.6.

Of course, a number of factors come into play in determining birth rates. Slow economic growth appears to be the modern paradigm, and couples are less likely to have children when their financial resources are strained. It is also the case that women today have much greater freedom to pursue a career than in previous eras. This latter factor is believed to explain a shift in the main childbearing years from the late teens and early twenties to the mid-thirties. That shift, understandably, has negative implications for family size.

However, as any parent of a teenager has learned, there is more to the story. A new option has arisen that spares young people the messy and awkward business of finding a mate. They can sit in their parent's basement and watch pornography on a computer screen. They can fire off illiterate e-mails to "friends" they rarely see in the flesh, and quite possibly prefer not to see at all. One study found that more than 40 percent of teenagers had sent or received a sexually suggestive message: "sexting." As for public spaces, their time there is taken up tweeting and texting instead of actually meeting someone. A sign in a café window that went viral reads: "We don't have Wi-Fi so you'll just have to talk to each other." Increasingly, our young adults simply do not know how to do that or at least are uncomfortable doing so.

At first blush, this all sounds implausible. How can young men possibly not know how to start a relationship with a woman? Since when do teenagers lack an interest in sex? Is this not biologically programmed into us? Is the urge to reproduce not the primary instinct of our species? Yet, we must consider the possibility that the answer to both of these questions is "no," or at least that it may be possible to override our biological programming if a powerful enough alternative presents itself. It is the thesis of this article and more generally of this book that such an alternative has arisen and that in the way we interact with it, our most basic sense of personhood can be altered. "Social media" is the preferred term for discussing this new presence in our lives, and by it we mean the Internet, cellphones, e-mail, texting, and other forms of electronic communication and information sharing.

It is scarcely a revelation that our perceptions can be influenced by visual media. Parents have been worrying for decades that overexposure to violence on television may encourage their children to experiment with the real thing. Women's groups have long argued that pornographic material in magazines and movies may exacerbate sexual misconduct in everyday life. The proposition I explore in this article is, in some ways, almost the reverse of these fears. Far from young adults being encouraged to mimic the behavior they see on television, I maintain that they are in fact led to withdraw from real life. Far from electronic pornography causing a rampage of aggressive male behavior toward women, I maintain that it is actually leading to the desexualization of young men. In effect, they do not want women at all, or at any rate, not in the flesh.

I believe social media induce these effects through a variety of mechanisms, among which the emergence of virtual reality technology plays a leading role. The term in itself is suggestive. By "virtual reality" we mean the growing ability, through computer-generated imagery, holography, and three-dimension technology, to present fictional scenes with such verisimilitude that they are difficult to distinguish from the real thing. Indeed, it is now often impossible to tell which parts of a movie are genuine and which were computer generated.

The original purpose behind this revolutionary capability was by no means sinister. It was simply to improve on the special effects of an earlier generation of movies and no more. Mere entertainment was the goal, and so it remains. We all understand that what we see in a movie theatre is just that—entertainment. We happily suspend our disbelief at the entrance and reactivate it upon leaving. But, this is an important point. We go to the theatre expecting to be entertained and we sit in an audience whose expectations and reactions mirror our own. We all laugh at the same scenes, recoil from the same scenes, cry at the same scenes. Yet, we know it is not real, as do those around us.

However, what happens when teenagers spend hour after hour in a basement or bedroom interacting with virtual reality is transformative. The power—and threat—of virtual reality is that it can, in a way, replicate the experiences of real life. In addition, it does so in complete isolation from real people and actual events. Here, in part, is why young Japanese men do not know how to relate to women. They simply do not have to. It is all there in front of them on a computer screen, or at least enough to be satisfying. Young men masturbating in front of a computer are not experiencing sex in its full sense, of course, but what they do experience is rewarding enough to serve as a substitute. Why risk the potential embarrassment and humiliation of refusal at the hands of a real woman when the screen version is endlessly compliant?

Young women suffer a different cause of withdrawal from normal sexual relations. Social media today are full of reported rape epidemics and other sexually violent behavior. For instance, there are 24-hour news reports that U.S. comedian Bill Cosby was a sexual predator, and that fraternity members at the University of Virginia engaged in the gang rape of a female student, and that players on the Duke University lacrosse team gang raped a young black woman on campus, and more of the same. Some of these allegations turn out to be false, but they are quickly replaced with new outrages. It would not be surprising if young women, confronted with this onslaught of alarming—indeed horrifying—evidence of sexual misconduct wanted nothing to do with men. Instead, through e-mails and texting, they establish circles of female contacts with whom they can maintain fragile but safe relationships—a virtual cocoon.

The second price paid for the emergence of social media is social isolation. Why go out into the real world if there is a believable and enjoyable alternate version right there on the screen? In earlier times, children read comic books and played with toys, which also offered a mild form of escapism, but one never sufficient to hold them for long. Friends beckoned; there were outdoor games to be played. That was what really mattered. Indeed, game playing with others was an important socializing mechanism in itself. It prepared children, in some of its aspects, for adulthood. It also prepared them for the world of work. A girl on a little league baseball team, who knows when it is her turn at bat and when it is not, has been taught an important lesson about self-control. A boy who has learned to win gracefully at football or soccer possesses an understanding that becomes useful later in life, when the wins and losses are for real.

By their very nature, social media are isolating. Partly, there is the time-consuming aspect of sending 3,000 texts a month. That certainly cuts into time spent with friends. There is also the solitude that surrounds this form of communication. Texting a friend demands one's full attention. Yet, the subject of that attention is not the friend; it is a screen atop a keypad. The process is more complicated in some important respects than casual face-to-face conversation. Texting engages those parts of the brain that manage hand and eye coordination. It is also dramatically narrower, insofar as one's entire focus is directed at an inanimate yet technologically sophisticated device. There are none of the visual and auditory cues that come with engaging a live person. Voice tone, facial mannerisms, body language, are all missing. Knowing when to speak and when to listen is not a factor. Gaging reactions and backing off when offense is taken plays no part. In addition, bullying is made infinitely easier, when the bully need never actually confront victims in the flesh.

These are not trivial matters. Human beings are a social species. We live in close proximity to one another, work together, play together, cooperate in meeting goals. It is essential that we know how to get along. How are young people to meet that need, when their primary form of intercommunication robs them of the very skills required? And what happens to their sense of self-worth, when the standard of the day is how many Facebook "friends" you boast?

It is not only the ability to understand and interact with others that is at stake, with the use of social media and texting in particular. There is precious little room for thoughtful self-reflection or quiet introspection in the world of instant texting. You pick up on a topic, bash out some garbled gibberish, and move on to the next message that demands your urgent attention. Aristotle reminded us that knowing yourself is the beginning of all wisdom. Today's younger generation is in danger of knowing only as much about themselves—or others—as can be condensed into a character-limited "tweet." The result is not the mindset of a sophisticated 21st-century urban dweller. It is closer to the impoverished world view of a 12th-century rural peasant. It seems improbable that such a reversion to the ignorance of earlier eras will fail to have some rather ugly consequences.

The third price I want to discuss is a diminution of language skills, and with that diminution, a loss of intellectual sophistication. Twitter and cellphone limitations on the number of characters a message may run makes technological sense. Longer messages use up bandwidth and flood small handheld screens. But abbreviation breeds an impoverished grasp of language—in both grammar and vocabulary. No doubt, adults long schooled in the breadth and depth of a given language survive without much damage, but teens and preteens whose language skills are not as well advanced face a higher risk of linguistic atrophy. They, in effect, no longer speak their native language but an abbreviated form of it.

It is difficult to predict how this phenomenon will continue to evolve. Youngsters have always used slang and local argots to talk among themselves. Previously, most of them either grew out of the practice naturally or were forced to do so by changing environments: from home to a university, the workplace, and so on. That they did grow out of the practice was at least in part because adult language has remained, up to now, of the non-abbreviated variety and youngsters of necessity had to adapt to it as they grew up. But social media use is not confined to youngsters. It is equally employed by adults. Will we see a diminished form of language use spread throughout broader lifestyles as the use of social media expands? That is certainly not an attractive prospect to contemplate.

The fourth price paid for social media use is the emerging realization that obsessive texting leads to changes in brain chemistry. Specifically, chemicals associated with substance abuse—cortisol, adrenaline, and dopamine—are all released when teens experience the rapid fire of texting. This may partly explain the enormous commitment of time and attention that teenagers are willing to devote to texting. They get a "high" from the sense of power and immediacy this technology produces. However, the same technology also breeds a generation of young people whose communication skills are poor, whose patience levels are minimal, and who lack the interest or staying power to take on more complex objectives. It seems reasonable to presume that loss of skills like these must have unfortunate employment-related consequences.

There are differences of opinion among psychologists as to whether texting and cellphone use should be classified as addictive. However, there is no dispute that these activities stimulate brain mechanisms associated with the fight-or-flee reflex, and also with feelings of intense pleasure and gratification. This may all be problematic at present, but the chemicals in question do cloud the brain's capacity for clear thinking and balanced judgment. That is, indeed, the primary role of adrenaline: to set aside measured deliberation and produce instant responses.

What is at issue here is akin to a form of sensory deprivation. A broad range of audiovisual and tactile experiences are replaced with a more limited but cleverly manipulated array of presentations that subtly alter the viewer's perceptions of reality over time. It is worth noting that the same technique has been used by state agencies to gain the compliance of detainees during interrogation. There, of course, the manipulation is deliberate. That is not the case with virtual reality; Hollywood is not deliberately trying to alter anyone's behavior. But that is part of the problem. What makes these consciousness-altering effects more troubling is precisely that they are both unintended and, in part at least, unremarked by those they affect. If we were dealing with deliberate manipulation, either by companies that manufacture social media devices or by the entertainment industry that produces virtual reality material, a hue and cry would ensue. We are perpetually on guard for such nefarious behavior by a corporate sector of which we are already suspicious. But virtual reality is not a deliberate attempt to manipulate our inner sense of self or our outward behavior. It flies under the radar precisely because it appears benign and even impressive. It affects our consciousness because we embrace it, not because some power imposed it upon us. This is the warning that Michel Foucault issued. The effects of new technology that should concern us most are those that were never intended. Hollywood did not mean to isolate teenagers in their basements. Apple never imagined its products would convert a generation of healthy young men into drones. Yet, this and much more has happened.

In short, social media confront us with a disembodied form of communication that results in social isolation, crude and primitive uses of language, likely alterations in brain chemistry, shorter attention spans, and a scary lack of self-awareness and meaningful knowledge of others. Moreover, we must not forget that the relevant technology is still, more or less, in its infancy. Text messaging is only two decades old. Digital cellular networks emerged in the early 1990s. If we take the industrial revolution as an analogy, texting and cellphones in their current manifestations are comparable to the invention of the steam engine: a development that had huge repercussions. The analogy can be extended: one consequence of the industrial revolution was the realization that modern worksites were far more squalid and dangerous places than had ever before been seen. Health and safety regulations were required to protect workers from the carnage that inadequately shielded heavy machinery could exact. Child labor had to be outlawed, once it became clear that employing children in a factory or a mine was an entirely different proposition than having them help out around the home or farm. Even so, the specter of the dark satanic mill lingered for a century and more before society drew a line.

How will we regulate the Internet? How will we prevent obsessive texting from dulling the minds of our children? There is no obvious answer. The unregulated nature of the Internet in comparison with the more manageable aspects of everyday life is, for many, one of its attractions.

There are devoted guardians of that freedom who will oppose any attempt at limiting its role and scope. And how, in any case, could we forestall the self-isolating use of cellphones and texting while preserving their undeniable advantages? There is an inexorable aspect to the advance of modern technology that bodes ill for any meaningful attempt to reverse its more problematic effects.

Of course, in one sense, we have been here before regarding this sort of change. Drawing-room conversation in a late 17th-century mansion was vastly more complex and formal than chitchat in a modern domestic setting. Classical music far exceeded in complexity its contemporary versions. Modern art, largely, is a pale shadow of Renaissance paintings. Then, it is probable that what we now take as troubling, personality-altering phenomena inherent in use of social media will look much less threatening 50 years from now, when the broader effects of the new technology have been absorbed and become routine and—if reflected on—are likely to be accepted as a welcome addition to human lives and experience and awareness of losses themselves lost.

The final price imposed by social media on society, in its broader sense, is a weakening of the foundations that civic life is built upon. It is a necessity of a liberal, democratic, and compassionate society that its members inform themselves about the affairs of the day. To take up their role both as contributors to and guardians of such a society, citizens must expend the time and effort to be knowledgeable about key events in the life of the community. That means being broadly aware of contemporary political and public policy issues, having at least some grasp of international trends, and staying abreast of developments in the domestic economy. In short, it means attempting to understand what is going on around one.

There is good reason, however, to doubt that this effort is being made, at least among younger people who are the heaviest users of the Internet and social media. Consider these findings by Statistics Canada: The proportion of young people who say they rarely or never follow current events doubled between 2003 and 2013. Only 37 percent of them now keep up with the news, compared to 81 percent of older Canadians. By almost 20 points, recent university graduates pay less attention to current affairs than senior citizens who never finished high school. And the cause, in part, is the rising presence of the Internet and social media. Nearly 80 percent of kids aged 15 to 34 now rely entirely on these sources for whatever knowledge of news and current events they possess.

Now, the arrival of social media and the Internet has been hailed as the dawn of a new era—the Information Age. This is supposedly a liberating development. Where once we worked with our hands, now we are free to use our minds. The limitless vistas provided by the Internet will open a broad new field of knowledge and enlightenment. Yet, as anyone familiar with the dreadful blather that passes for informed comment on Twitter and Facebook knows, this is not where things are headed. Indeed, it would be tempting to rename our period in history the Disinformation Age.

Yet arguably that misses a key function of social media. Its purpose is not, in the main, to inform or enlighten us. Its purpose is to amuse and titillate us. Like the Circus Maximus in ancient Rome, the Internet offers primarily entertainment in the form of gory violence, sex, rumor and vitriol. It is, if anything, a form of escape from the humdrum of daily life, not a source of personal betterment or a means of thoughtful civic involvement. Kids who get their news from blogs or websites instead of reading newspapers or watching televised public affairs shows are in fact tuning out, not tuning in. They are more likely to hold distorted or biased views about issues of the day, because their sources of information are, in the main, undigested, unedited, and generally unreliable.

I suspect a case could be made that the rise of Donald Trump in the political life of our neighboring republic reflected, in part, this specific form of impoverishment. His bromides and gauzy generalizations matched exactly the mindset of his audience. In effect, he turned a political contest into a form of TV reality show. Pundits and commentators put this down to Trump's bizarre personality and narcissism. But what matters for our discussion is that it worked—at least for a time. Many Americans admired his simplistic and even boorish message. It is difficult to imagine such a phenomenon, say, 40 years ago.

In short, far from ushering in an age of enlightenment, there is reason to believe that the advent of the Internet and social media have cheapened political discourse, deprived many younger people of even a basic knowledge of public affairs, and in the process, weakened our civic fabric.

A century has passed since J. M. Barrie wrote *Peter Pan*. He intended the book, of course, to be a work of fiction. However, today, in households throughout the developed world, "the boy who wouldn't grow up" is far from a fictional entity. He is, indeed, the new reality: self-absorbed, isolated, desexualized, uninformed, and wholly lacking the social skills required to becoming a socially effective and companionable adult. If we are not careful, a fictional Neverland may become our roadmap to the future.

A Different Kind of Price Paid for Electronic Communication

The second part of this article deals with a different kind of price we pay for electronic connectivity and social media, specifically: some of the ways in which electronic communications have invaded the workplace with destructive effects.

Hillary Clinton's e-mail crisis is as good a place to start as any. Clinton, it will be recalled, elected to store on her home computer a large number of official e-mail files while she was U.S. Secretary of State. Though her reasons are obscure, a not implausible hypothesis is that she wished to retain personal control of the material. Perhaps, as President Richard Nixon intended when he installed a covert tape recording system in the Oval Office, her purpose was to create an archive on which she could draw at a later date to write her memoirs. Other, less innocent reasons have been suggested.

When it became known she had acted in this manner, Clinton had roughly half of the e-mails stored on her computer—some 30,000—wiped by a company that specializes in such matters. The remainder she turned over to the State Department. At the time of this writing, various investigative agencies are examining Clinton's server and other devices to see if the scrubbed files can be recovered. But regardless of the outcome, the effect of her decision was to remove from the public record a large body of material, some of which may have had historical significance.

Clinton's is perhaps an extreme case, yet it is in the nature of electronic communications that they are more easily manipulated, concealed, and if necessary destroyed than traditional paper records. This fact has serious consequences for the entire apparatus through which corporations and governments are held accountable, scrutinized, and in the case of governments, evaluated after they leave office. Consider public sector websites. It is not uncommon for both the federal government and either state or provincial administrations to post policy proposals on their websites. These postings remain entirely at the discretion of the governments who place them on their website. They can be amended, expanded, and if necessary or thought expedient, deleted with no record remaining.

Nor is it only governments and companies whose actions can be camouflaged by these means. Individual public servants and corporate executives also may find it profitable to conduct their business electronically rather than by the traditional method. It is now understood at senior levels of management that written paper communications are to be avoided where possible. "Don't put it on paper," goes the saying, unless you want to read it on the front page of a newspaper. Of course, the policy of conducting even the most important business by limited access e-mail deprives lower-level managers of an opportunity to read and understand their agency's intentions. In this sense, e-mails of this sort are a form of private language. The threat to accountability is magnified by the option, available on Blackberry devices, of sending e-mails that will not register on government data banks and that can be erased without trace. By this means, government officials can exchange notes that no one else will see and government policies about preserving electronic communications are unenforceable.

Now, let us consider for a moment what the "traditional" method of communication and record keeping within governments entailed. A senior manager in the Health department or ministry, who wished to raise a proposal with a colleague in the Justice Ministry or department, would give instructions to her or his secretary, who produced a written memo for the manager's signature and kept a record of it in a daily log. That memo was then routed through the hands of mail clerks to the Justice Ministry. There, a second secretary would open the envelope, create a corresponding log entry that identified the author of the memo and its content, and then place it in his or her manager's inbox. Any response would follow the same process in reverse. The result was a paper trail that would be difficult to eradicate completely. At a minimum, several people, some of them clerical staff, would have to be brought into any such decision to eradicate the memo. The strengths of such a procedure speak for themselves. A chain of custody is created that would be difficult to conceal in the investigation of and aftermath discussion of some scandal or alleged wrongdoing. Alleged participants would have to tread carefully regarding what they claimed since their original messages could surface at any time.

Moreover, governments at federal, state or provincial, and municipal levels maintain legislative libraries where print records are maintained by professional staff. These libraries are essential both for the preservation of records and the roles played by their staffs. Librarians will see to it that proper archives are maintained and they are, in effect, the collective memory of the departments and ministries of state. If nothing else, these records are of inestimable value to historians. Of course, this practice is only viable if records are laid down in the first place and in a manner that permits their preservation.

E-mails, by contrast, leave no paper trails and require no clerical involvement. One of the corollaries of the electronic age is that virtually every employee, from the most junior to the most senior, now types. There was a time when typing was a skill unknown to most executives. This is a mostly unremarked phenomenon, but it has radically altered the handling of government and private sector business. Clerical staff was until recently a vital link in the machinery through which correspondence was routed. Their presence in a manager's office brought formal process into play. Secretarial resources are still required, but now mostly for low-level work such as answering the phone and maintaining meeting calendars. Most high-level communications are now more likely to be handled by the managers themselves, using keyboards that an earlier generation of executives would have disdained from using. This shifting of clerical staff to the periphery of office regimes has played a role in greatly denuding the process of interagency communications, and thereby undermining recordkeeping and with it accountability.

Nor is it only public oversight of governments and corporations that is diminished. In 2014, the European Court of Justice ordered Google to let users erase records of their Internet history. The court was concerned that online search engines can reveal more about a person's private affairs than may be warranted. That certainly is true. Everything from divorce hearings to allegations of child abuse, to say nothing of mortgages and current bank balances can be discovered by trolling through the Internet, and occasionally paying some website a modest fee for greater detail.

Some of this material may be damaging in the extreme to personal reputations. Consider, for example, the harm a person may suffer if it becomes known that he or she has been charged with a crime. Though there has been no trial and the presumption of innocence supposedly applies, the embarrassment caused by a premature revelation of this kind may well exceed whatever statutorily prescribed punishment is involved. This scenario has brought about the rise of an entire industry of fly-by-night companies in the United States who promise, for a fee, to remove a person's name and mug shot from law enforcement websites. As often as not, the promise is not honored, and instead the client finds his or her computer barraged with viruses, malware, and spyware applications. Yet, as critics of the Google ruling also pointed out, the Internet is a valuable repository of information that society may require. If a politician running for office has a history of criminal convictions, for instance, is that not something we should know? If a businessperson has a record of numerous bankruptcies, is that not something of which potential shareholders should be aware?

In both arenas, government and the corporate sector, history now can be rewritten or submerged in ways that almost certainly do not comport with the public interest. It may be argued that this development is scarcely a novel situation. Vital records have been deliberately destroyed down the ages. Often, a convenient fire, or a flood, or other natural disaster was blamed. However, the unique aspect of electronic data is the immediacy and relative ease with which it can be simply and wiped away without trace. If we assume that human nature has remained essentially unchanged over time, we must also assume that the desire to cover one's tracks, especially if those tracks lead somewhere unpleasant, is ever with us.

What should be done is another matter. Most cyber experts today believe that, essentially, any electronic database can be hacked. Public bodies often have rigorous protocols for the storage and preservation of electronic data—though Hillary Clinton's case illustrates the dangers of putting our trust on such protocols. Regardless of protocols, though, an insurmountable difficulty remains: e-mails and other computer files have an electronic half-life that can be limited, if desired, to seconds. No electronic archival system, regardless of the effort spent in building it, can prevent files simply disappearing into the ether if programmed to do so. We are dealing here with a different kind of Neverland—a domain in which vital records can vanish as if they had never existed.

Afterword

Realizing the Consequences of Internet and Social Media Usage

Bruce MacNaughton

Michel Foucault once said, commenting on causality and unintended consequences, "People know what they do; frequently they know why they do what they do; but what they don't know is what what they do does."[1]

In the past number of years, I have come to appreciate the astuteness of that remark as it applies to the legal system. A natural consequence of the pervasive nature of the internet and the degree to which people's lives are "lived" online is the rise in the use of social media evidence in the investigation and prosecution of criminal cases. As a Crown Prosecutor (primarily, a drugs prosecutor, but many other criminal charges as well), I have found the use of social media evidence invaluable.

The legendary Van Morrison sang, "All is lost carelessly." Teens and preteens, aside from walking into vehicles whilst texting, unknowingly produce evidence for the police and eventual criminal charges. For example, young persons will proudly post pictures of themselves on Facebook, Instagram, and so forth, displaying their weapons, stores of methamphetamine, MDMA (Ecstasy), cocaine, and marijuana. They even post pictures of themselves during a break and enter or a home invasion, seemingly thinking it is merely anonymous braggadocio. It is decidedly not.

If an individual is known to a police force to be involved in criminal activity, an officer will very early on in an investigation go to the Internet to observe what that person's presence there is and will use that information to further the investigation.

"Look at me, look at me," has become an irresistible habit. And, it is assumed that there are no consequences. However, there surely are consequences. I dare say that if there was actual face-to-face communication, one of the young person's pals might say, "What the hell are you doing? Stop it!" Then again, perhaps not. But the presumption or ignorance that everything online—text, photos—is private is drastically and dangerously mistaken.

Frequently, and as recently as within two weeks of this writing, a young person chose to post a picture on Facebook. He decided he would pose with two semi-automatic pistols. He was then subjected to a weapons prohibition charge pursuant to the Criminal Code of Canada. His posting came, not surprisingly, to the attention of the local police force, and he was investigated and arrested. Now, this young person manifestly has issues. One cannot say that social media alone led to his difficulties; however, one thing is clear: those difficulties were certainly brought to light through social media.

I shall not address the socioeconomic issues behind a young person's criminal activity; it is not my purview. What is astounding is that young persons want to brag about what they are up to for the world to see. Clearly, people, especially young persons, want attention and need to talk. That is human nature. We, as prosecutors, rely on that. Any defense counsel advises his or her client to not say anything when interviewed by the police. Almost invariably, they do. There may be issues and challenges around the matter of whether defense counsels' clients' statements were spontaneous or voluntary utterances during an investigation, arrest, booking, or interview, of course. But texts or pictures posted on various forms of social media, being public, provide ready and incontrovertible evidence for the Crown.

It is perfectly normal for a person to say to his or her friends at a party or gathering, "C'mere, I gotta show you what I got." That has always happened. But social media have raised such impulsive actions to a different level: they are there for all the world to see and anonymity is not realized.

Many people use the same technology in the course of their professional lives. I do. My colleagues have often called me a "heat seeker"—someone who always wants the latest technology. I confess that I do because I use it. It is a tool. It is a part of the job. I use it when I need it. Frequently. But I do not use it compulsively. I do not text someone to say, "I'm at the delicatessen now, where are you?" It is more likely to be, "Are you surveilling so-and-so presently and what stage is the investigation at?" Or I might contact my staff when I am in a courtroom to enquire whether we have a previous brief on someone who is in Bail Court at that moment. It is a technological convenience; now, almost a technological necessity.

That said, the compulsive way in which many young people use the same technology leads one to think that they use it as a means of avoiding personal face-to-face contact while still "communicating." Or they use it as a way to pursue criminal activity, to threaten, or to further their enterprises, seemingly without harm or consequences. After all, it is just a text or picture. Little do they know that their texts and image postings to various social media sites are an open book to investigators.

It is the illusory anonymity that traps one.

In the recent past, prosecutors and police agencies have been able to obtain Production Orders from cellular service providers, which provide a transcript of every single past text message written by an individual for the time period requested. While the providers did not relish these orders, they produced what is essentially a wiretap, without the need of a wiretap order. Every single text written and received is laid out. For example, "You got any white today?" "Yeah bud, meet me at . . ."

Certainly, obtaining prospective communications would require a warrant pursuant to the Criminal Code (Part VI). In the past, providers would keep all messages. Currently, some providers keep communications for approximately 30 days, others do not retain them. Previously, all carriers kept them for roughly 150 days. However, when a person is arrested now and is in possession of a cell phone, a warrant may be obtained to view its entire contents.

Pulitzer Prize winning author Matt Richtel wrote *A Deadly Wandering*, a book that examines the impact of texting and driving: a book that examines the impact of technology on our lives. It tells the story of a Utah college student who, in 2006, as a result of texting while driving killed two scientists. In an interview on CBC's "The Current," the student provides very interesting and provocative insights. He likens the need to respond to a text to one of our ancestors responding to a tap on the shoulder. Is this a friend or foe? One must know, and one must know now. As is noted in some of the articles that follow, a text now demands the same response. I must know and respond—immediately—and technology provides the ability to do so, no matter the circumstances or surroundings. The (former) student is now one of the leading advocates against distracted driving.

The world is addicted to technology. How did I ever practice law without a computer or a cell phone? I graduated without one in philosophy and subsequently law without one. Presently, I use two smartphones. Each of my staff has a cellphone. I have two computers on my desk; each of my staff members—four—has two computers. However, they are tools. I do not text and contact an acquaintance to say, "I'm at the pizza shop.

Where are you?" When I text, it is a protected message to officers with respect to an investigation or an ongoing matter. Most professionals do as I do—they use cellphones and computers as tools, as part of the job. We may use computers and cellphones frequently, but not compulsively. Cellphones and computers are technological conveniences and fast becoming technological necessities.

From the perspective of a Crown Attorney, I would say again: one is not invisible when one uses social media and cellphones. We can and will use evidence found on both to prove our cases.

Note

1. Hubert Dreyfus and Paul Rabinow, *Michel Foucault: Beyond Structuralism and Hermeneutics*, 2nd edition with an Afterword by Michel Foucault (Chicago: University of Chicago Press, 1983), 187.

Bibliography

Ainslie, G. *Breakdown of Will*. Cambridge: Cambridge University Press, 2001.

Alba, Davey. "Facebook Tests Emoji Reactions to Fix Its 'Dislike' Problem." *Wired* (October 8, 2015). http://www.wired.com/2015/10/facebook-reaction-emoji/.

Alloway, T., and R. Alloway. "Attentional Control and Engagement with Digital Technology." *Nature Precedings* (January 2011). http://precedings.nature.com/documents/5603/version/1.

Alloway, T., and R. Alloway. "The Impact of Engagement with Social Networking Sites (SNSs) on Cognitive Skills." *Computers in Human Behavior* 28, no. 5 (2012): 1748–1754. http://www.sciencedirect.com/science/article/pii/S0747563212001197.

Aristotle. *Nicomachean Ethics*. Translated by Terence Irwin. Indianapolis: Hackett Publications, 1985.

Baddeley, A. *Working Memory, Thought, and Action*. New York: Oxford University Press, 2007.

Barrett, Lisa Feldman. "Psychological Construction: A Darwinian Approach to the Science of Emotion." *Emotion Review* 5, no. 4 (2013): 379–389.

Barwick, A. *Status Update: Celebrity, Publicity and Branding in the Social Media Age*. New Haven, CT: Yale University Press, 2013.

Benjamin, Walter. *Illuminations: Essays and Reflections*. Edited by Hannah Arendt. Translated by Harry Zohn. New York: Schocken Books, 1968.

Bermúdez, J. P. "Do We Reflect When Performing Skillful Actions?" *Automaticity, Control, and the Perils of Distraction*. Forthcoming.

Bower, Bruce. "Main Result of Facebook Emotion Study." *Science News* (July 3, 2014). https://www.sciencenews.org/blog/scicurious/main-result-facebook-emotion-study-less-trust-facebook

Boyd, D. *It's Complicated: The Social Lives of Networked Teens*. New Haven, CT: Yale University Press, 2014.

Bromwich, Jonah. "Essena O'Neill. 'Instagram Star, Recaptions Her Life.'" *New York Times* (November 03, 2015). http://www.nytimes.com/2015/11/04/fashion/essena-oneill-instagram-star-recaptions-her-life.html?_r=0.

Brownstein, M. "Rationalizing Flow: Agency in Skilled Unreflective Action." *Philosophical Studies* 168, no. 2 (2014): 545–568.

Butterfield, H. *The Whig Interpretation of History.* New York: W.W. Norton, 1965.

Canuel, Eric, director. *Bon Cop, Bad Cop.* Canada: Alliance Atlantis Vivafilm, 2006.

Carr, Nicholas. *The Shallows: What the Internet Is Doing to Our Brains.* New York: W.W. Norton, 2011.

Constine, Josh. "Compassion Researcher Helps Facebook's Apps Get Emotional with Animated Stickers." *Tech Crunch.* http://techcrunch.com/2013/04/26/facebook-animated-stickers/.

Cornell University. "A Revealing Look at Hidden Rites." hazing.cornell.edu. (n.d.). Retrieved May 5, 2016, from https://hazing.cornell.edu/.

Cuddy, Amy. "Your iPhone Is Ruining Your Posture—and Your Mood." *New York Times*, Sunday Review, December 12, 2015. http://www.nytimes.com/2015/12/13/opinion/sunday/your-iphone-is-ruining-your-posture-and-your-mood.html?_r=0.

Davies, Will. *The Happiness Industry: How Government and Big Business Sold Us Well-Being.* London, UK: Verso Books, 2015.

de Ridder, D. T., G. Lensvelt-Mulders, C. Finkenauer, F. M. Stok, and R. F. Baumeister. "Taking Stock of Self-Control: A Meta-Analysis of How Trait Self-Control Relates to a Wide Range of Behaviors." *Personality and Social Psychology Review* 16, no. 1 (2012): 76–99.

de Sousa, Ronald. "Emotion." In *Stanford Encyclopedia of Philosophy.* Edited by Zalta En. http://plato.stanford.edu/archives/spr2014/entries/emotion/.

Dewey, John. *Human Nature and Conduct: An Introduction to Social Psychology.* New York: The Modern Library, 1930.

Dewey, John. "Experience and Education." In *John Dewey: The Later Works, 1925–1953*, edited by Jo Ann Boydston. Vol. 13, 1–62. Carbondale: Southern Illinois University Press, 1988.

Dreyfus, H., and S. D. Kelly. "Heterophenomenology: Heavy-Handed Sleight-of-Hand." *Phenomenology and the Cognitive Sciences* 6, no. 1–2 (2007): 45–55.

Dreyfus, H. L. "Intelligence without Representation—Merleau-Ponty's Critique of Mental Representation. The Relevance of Phenomenology to Scientific Explanation." *Phenomenology and the Cognitive Sciences* 1, no. 4 (2002): 367–383.

Dreyfus, Hubert, and Paul Rabinow. *Michel Foucault: Beyond Structuralism and Hermeneutics.* 2nd ed. Chicago: University of Chicago Press, 1983.

durianrider. "How I Overcome Suicidal Depression." YouTube video. April 26, 2014. https://www.youtube.com/watch?v=cwpcP5-Iuko.

durianrider. "Essena Oneill Quits Uni Cos of Us." YouTube video. June 21, 2015. https://www.youtube.com/watch?v=79vVNvPzU2I.

Dutton, Denis. "Freedom and the Theatre of Ideas." Address to the Russian Institute of Aesthetics. January 1990. http://denisdutton.com/moscow_address.htm.

Facebook Newsroom. "Highlights from Q&A with Mark." September 15, 2015. http://newsroom.fb.com/news/2015/09/highlights-from-qa-with-mark-8/.

Foucault, Michel. *Discipline and Punish: The Birth of the Prison.* Translated by Alan Sheridan. New York: Pantheon, 1979.

Frankfurt, H. G. "Freedom of the Will and the Concept of a Person." *The Journal of Philosophy* 68, no.1 (1971): 5–20.

Freelee the Banana Girl. "Anorexia, Bulimia, Part 2 My Recovery Freelee's Story." YouTube video. May 17, 2012. https://www.youtube.com/watch?v= 9pp7Jm1G50k.

Fridland, E. "They've Lost Control: Reflections on Skill." *Synthese* 191, no. 12 (2014): 2729–2750.

Gladwell, M. "Small Change: Why the Revolution Will Not Be Tweeted." *New Yorker,* October 4, 2010. http://www.newyorker.com/magazine/2010/10/04/ small-change-malcolm-gladwell.

Gladwell, M. "The Coolhunt." *New Yorker,* March 17, 1997. Retrieved May 05, 2016 from http://www.newyorker.com/magazine/1997/03/17/the-coolhunt.

Goldberg, Michelle. "The Democratic Party Ruined My Friendship!" *Slate,* April 2016. http://www.slate.com/articles/news_and_politics/poli- tics/2016/04/the_democratic_primary_ruined_my_friendship.html.

Gould, Steven J., and Richard Charles Lewontin. "The Spandrels of San Marco and the Panglossian Paradigm: A Critique of the Adaptationist Pro- gramme." *Proceedings of the Royal Society.* London Series B 205, no. 11 (1979): 581–598.

Greene, Maxine. *Dialectic of Freedom.* New York: Teachers' College Press, 1988.

Grindstaff, Laura, and Susan Murray. "Reality Celebrity: Branded Affect and the Emotion Economy." *Public Culture* 27, no. 1 75 (2015): 109–135.

Heath, J. *Enlightenment 2.0: Restoring Sanity to Our Politics, Our Economy, and Our Lives.* Toronto: HarperCollins, 2014.

Heath, J., and J. Anderson. "Procrastination and the Extended Will." In *The Thief of Time: Philosophical Essays on Procrastination,* edited by C. Andreou and M. D. White. 233–253. New York: Oxford University Press, 2010.

Hobsbawm, E. J. *Primitive Rebels.* Manchester: The University Press, 1959.

Holmes, Su. "All You've Got to Worry About Is the Task, Having a Cup of Tea, and Doing a Bit of Sunbathing: Approaching Celebrity in Big Brother." In *Understanding Reality Television,* edited by Su Holmes and Deborah Jer- myn. 111–135. London: Routledge, 2004.

Hunt, Elle. "Essena O'Neill Quits Instagram Claiming Social Media 'Is Not Real Life'". *The Guardian,* November 3, 2015. http://www.theguardian.com/ media/2015/nov/03/instagram-star-essena-oneill-quits-2d-life-to- reveal-true-story-behind-images.

Kaplan, Andreas M., and Michael Haenlein. "Users of the World, Unite! The Challenges and Opportunities of Social Media." *Business Horizons* 53, no. 1 (2010): 61.

Karpinski, A. C., P. A. Kirschner, I. Ozer, J. A. Mellott, and P. Ochwo. "An Explo- ration of Social Networking Site Use, Multitasking, and Academic Perfor- mance among United States and European University Students." *Computers in Human Behavior* 29, no. 3 (2013): 1182–1192.

Keating, C. F., J. Pomerantz, S. D. Pommer, S. J. Ritt, L. M. Miller, and J. Mccormick. "Going to College and Unpacking Hazing: A Functional Approach to Decrypting Initiation Practices among Undergraduates." *Group Dynamics: Theory, Research, and Practice* 9, no. 2, 104–126. DOI:10.1037/1089–2699.9.2.104.

Kramer, Adam D., Jamie E. Guillory, and Jeffery T. Hancock. "Experimental Evidence of Massive-Scale Emotional Contagion through Social Networks." *Proceedings of the National Academy of Sciences* 111, no. 24 (2014): 8788–8790. DOI: 10.1073/pnas.1320040111.

L'Hermitte, F. "'Utilization Behaviour' and Its Relation to Lesions of the Frontal Lobes." *Brain* 106 (1983): 237–255.

Laakmann, G. 150 Programming Interview Questions and Solutions. *CareerCup*, 2011.

Lang, Nico. "45 Hilariously Relatable Jenna Marbles Quotes That Are Words to Live By." *ThoughtCatalog.* http://thoughtcatalog.com/nico-lang/2013/08/45-hilariously-relatable-jenna-marbles-quotes-that-are-words-to-live-by/.

Larson, Q. "Why Is Hiring Broken? It Starts at The Whiteboard." *Free Code Camp.* Retrieved May 05, 2016, from https://medium.freecodecamp.com/why-is-hiring-broken-it-starts-at-the-whiteboard-34b088e5a5db#.4yy1n6r2w.

Laurenson, L. "My Year in San Francisco's $2 Million Secret Society Startup." *Motherboard.* Retrieved May 05, 2016, from http://motherboard.vice.com/read/my-year-in-san-franciscos-2-million-secret-society-startup.

Lin, L. "Breadth-Biased versus Focused Cognitive Control in Media Multitasking Behaviors." *Proceedings of the National Academy of Sciences* 106, no. 37 (2009): 15521–15522.

Lupton, Deborah. "'Feeling Better Connected': Academics' Use of Social Media." Report published by News and Media Research Centre, University of Canberra, 2014.

Lutz, Catherine. *Unnatural Emotions: Everyday Sentiments on a Micronesian Atoll.* Chicago: University of Chicago Press, 1988.

Marbles, Jenna. "How to Trick People into Thinking You're Good Looking." YouTube video. July 9, 2010. https://www.youtube.com/watch?v=OYpwAtnywTk.

Marbles, Jenna. "Oh Great Job Good Morning America." Jenna Marbles blog post. April 22, 2013. http://jennamarblesblog.com/oh-great-job-good-morning-america/.

Marche, Stephen. "Is Facebook Making Us Lonely?" Quoting John Cacioppo, Director of the Center for Cognitive and Social Neuroscience, University of Chicago. *The Atlantic* (May 2012): 60–69.

Marquina, Sierra. "Miley Cyrus Doesn't Need a 'Squad' Like Taylor Swift, Has Normal Friends: 'I Just Like Real People.'" *US Weekly*, August 31, 2015. http://www.usmagazine.com/celebrity-news/news/miley-cyrus-doesnt-need-a-squad-like-taylor-swift-has-normal-friends-2015318.

Marwick, Alice. *Status Update: Celebrity, Publicity and Branding in the Social Media Age.* New Haven, CT: Yale University Press, 2013.

Marwick, Alice, and Dana Boyd. "I Tweet Honestly, I Tweet Passionately: Twitter Users, Context Collapse, and the Imagined Audience." *New Media & Society* XX, no. X (July 7, 2010): 1–20.

McCall, Jennifer. "Jenna Marbles' Tweets are Hilariously Relatable." *The Berry*, February 26, 2015. http://theberry.com/2015/02/26/jenna-marbles-tweets-are-hilariously-relatable-20-photos/.

McGilchrist, Iain. *The Master and His Emissary.* New Haven and London: Yale University Press, 2012.

McLuhan, M. *Understanding Media: The Extensions of Man.* New York: McGraw Hill, 1964.

McLuhan, Marshall, Quentin Fiore, and Jerome Agel. *The Medium Is the Message: An Inventory of Effects.* New York: Bantam Books, 1967.

Microsoft Canada. "Attention spans." *Consumer Insights.* Microsoft Canada, 2015.

Mischel, W. and E. B. Ebbesen. "Attention in Delay of Gratification." *Journal of Personality and Social Psychology* 16, no. 2 (1970): 329.

Mischel, W., E. B. Ebbesen, and A. Raskoff Zeiss. "Cognitive and Attentional Mechanisms in Delay of Gratification." *Journal of Personality and Social Psychology* 21, no. 2 (1972): 204.

Montero, B. G. *The Myth of 'Just Do It': Thought and Effort in Expert Action.* Oxford: Oxford University Press. Forthcoming.

Ophir, E., C. Nass, and A. D. Wagner. "Cognitive Control in Media Multitaskers." *Proceedings of the National Academy of Sciences* 106, no. 37 (2009): 15583–15587.

Paglieri, F. "Ulysses' Will: Self-Control, External Constraints, and Games." In *Consciousness in Interaction: The Role of the Natural and Social Context in Shaping Consciousness*, edited F. Paglieri and John Benjamins. *Advances in Consciousness Research* 86 (2012): 179–206. doi: 10.1075/aicr.86.10pag.

Pandey, S., and N. Sarma. "Utilization Behavior." *Annals of Indian Academy of Neurology* 18, no. 2 (2015): 235.

Pew Research Center. "Teens, Technology and Friendships." August 6, 2015. www.pewresearch.org.

Pnw_smalls. "Sorority Girls at a Baseball Game." *Reddit*, October 1, 2015. https://www.reddit.com/r/videos/comments/3n3m2d/sorority_girls_at_a_baseball_game.

Rabin, Toni Caryn. "Compulsive Texting Takes Toll on Teenagers." *New York Times*, October 12, 2015. www.well.blogs.nytimes.com.

Rieber, L. P., L. Smith, L., and D. Noah. "The Value of Serious Play." *Educational Technology* 38, no. 6 (1998): 29–37.

Rietveld, E. "Context-Switching and Responsiveness to Real Relevance." In *Heidegger and Cognitive Science*, edited by J. Kiverstein and M. Wheeler. 105–135. Basingstoke, Hants: Palgrave Macmillan, 2012.

Romano, Aja. "Hank Green on Why 'GMA' Has Jenna Marbles All Wrong." *The Daily Dot*, April 23, 2013. http://www.dailydot.com/entertainment/hank-green-jenna-marbles-good-morning-america/.

Rouis, S., M. Limayem, and E. Salehi-Sangari. "Impact of Facebook Usage on Students' Academic Achievement: Role of Self-Regulation and Trust." *Electronic Journal of Research in Educational Psychology* 9, no. 3 (2011): 961–994.

Saiidi, Upton. "Social Media Making Millennials Less Social: Study." CNBC, October 17, 2015. http://www.cnbc.com/2015/10/15/social-media-making-millennials-less-social-study.html.

Sales, Nancy Jo. *American Girls: Social Media and the Secret Lives of Teenagers*. New York: Borzoi Books, Alfred Knopf, 2016.

Schlam, T. R., N. L. Wilson, Y. Shoda, W. Mischel, and O. Ayduk. "Preschoolers' Delay of Gratification Predicts their Body Mass 30 Years Later." *The Journal of Pediatrics* 162, no. 1 (2013): 90–93.

Shea, Courtney. "10 Posts You Can't Wait to Dislike on Facebook # Truth." *Flare*, September 25, 2015. http://www.flare.com/celebrity/entertainment/10-posts-you-cant-wait-to-dislike-on-facebook/.

Shoda, Y., W. Mischel, and P. K. Peake. "Predicting Adolescent Cognitive and Self-Regulatory Competencies from Preschool Delay of Gratification: Identifying Diagnostic Conditions." *Developmental Psychology* 26, no. 6 (1990): 978.

Simon, Herbert. "Designing Organizations for an Information-Rich World." In *Computers, Communication and the Public Interest*, edited by M. Greenberger. 32–71. Baltimore, MD: The John Hopkins Press, 1969.

Simons, D. J., and C. F. Chabris. "Gorillas in Our midst: Sustained Inattentional Blindness for Dynamic Events." *Perception* 28, no. 9 (1999): 1059–1074.

Sullivan, Gail. "Sheryl Sandberg Not Sorry for Facebook Mood Manipulation Study." *Washington Post*, July 3, 2014. http://www.washingtonpost.com/news/morning-mix/wp/2014/07/03/sheryl-sandberg-not-sorry-for-facebook-mood-manipulation-study/.

Tsukayama, Hayley. "This Dark Side of the Internet Is Costing Young People Their Jobs and Social Lives." *The Washington Post* Business Section, May 20, 2016.

Turkle, Sherry. *Alone Together: Why We Expect More from Technology and Less from Each Other*. New York: Basic Books, 2011.

Turner, Fred. *From Counterculture to Cyberculture: Stewart Brand, the Whole Earth Network, and the Rise of Digital Utopianism*. Chicago: University of Chicago Press, 2010.

Turner, Graeme. "The Mass Production of Celebrity: Celetoids, Reality TV, and the 'Demotic Turn.'" *International Journal of Cultural Studies* 9, no. 2 (2006): 153–165.

Turner, Graeme. *Ordinary People and the Media: The Demotic Turn*. London: Sage, 2010.

Tversky, A., and D. Kahneman. "The Framing of Decisions and the Psychology of Choice." *Science* 211, no. 4481 (1981): 453–458.

Weisberg, Jacob. "We Are Hopelessly Hooked." *New York Review of Books*, February 25, 2016. http://www.nybooks.com/articles/2016/02/25/we-are-hopelessly-hooked/.

Wilcox, K., and A. T. Stephen. "Are Close Friends the Enemy? Online Social Networks, Self-Esteem, and Self-Control." *Journal of Consumer Research* 40, no. 1 (2013): 90–103.

Wittgenstein, Ludwig. *Philosophical Investigations.* Translated by G. E. M. Anscombe. Oxford: Basil Blackwell, 1958.

About the Editor and Contributors

C. G. Prado, PhD, FRSC, is Emeritus Professor of Philosophy, Queen's University, a Fellow of the Royal Society, and listed in *Who's Who in Canada*. He has authored, coauthored, and edited 18 books on religion, Descartes, Michel Foucault, and assisted suicide. His most recent books are *Starting with Descartes* and *Coping with Choices to Die*. He has also contributed to a number of collections and published numerous journal papers (www.cgprado.com).

Chris Beeman, PhD, is Assistant Professor of Education at Brandon University. His research includes long-term friendships and research relationships with Teme Augama Anishinaabe and other aboriginal elders in exploring the connection between human beings and their physical locale through the growing and gathering of food.

Juan Pablo Bermúdez, PhD, teaches philosophy at the Universidad Externado de Colombia. His work bridges the classical Greek tradition of Plato and Aristotle and contemporary issues at the intersection between philosophy and psychology. His current focus is on deciphering the philosophical implications of empirical research on the human mind, and what we can learn from them to lead more autonomous and authentic lives. He has written and lectured on topics such as the nature of automatic behavior, the limitations of our decision-making capacities, and what we can do to overcome them.

Khadija Coxon holds degrees in English and Philosophy and is a writer, researcher, and editor working in Toronto. She has written extensively on philosophical issues around emotions, aesthetics, and food. She currently edits articles for *Social Studies of Science*, manages the journal's official

Twitter account, and likes to keep in touch online with members of a community of hobby bakers @amorouspanivore.

Paul Fairfield, PhD, is Professor of Philosophy at Queen's University. He is the author of several books on hermeneutics, existential phenomenology, and the philosophy of education, including *Death: A Philosophical Inquiry, Philosophical Hermeneutics Reinterpreted, Education After Dewey,* and *Teachability and Learnability* (forthcoming; www.paulfairfield.com).

Mark Kingwell, MLitt, MPhil, PhD, DFA, is Professor of Philosophy at the University of Toronto and a contributing editor of *Harper's Magazine* in New York. He is the author or coauthor of 18 books of political, cultural, and aesthetic theory. In addition to many scholarly articles, his writings have appeared in more than 40 mainstream magazines and newspapers. His recent books are the essay collections *Unruly Voices* (2012) and *Measure Yourself Against the Earth* (2015).

Alex Leitch, BA (Hon), MDes, is a systems developer and creative technologist in Toronto, Omtario. Cofounder of Site 3 coLaboratory and Dames Making Games, Alex is well known in the Toronto "maker" community for organizing makerspaces. She is a member of the Banff Centre's 2016 Lougheed Leadership program and has won a variety of scholarships and awards for her work in the future of contemporary art and system design. She has presented on the topics of rapid prototyping, video game design, group management, and retail organization in Canada (http://alexleitch.com).

Bruce MacNaughton, BA (Hon), LLB/JD, is a Crown Attorney and runs his own law firm. He was called to the Ontario Bar in 1983, and was a partner in the Johnston and MacNaughton firm, focusing on family law, before becoming a sole practitioner. He is a Deputy Judge of the Superior Court of Justice (Small Claims Court). The bulk of his work is in Crown Prosecutions and agency work for the Department of Justice. MacNaughton has lectured in business law at St. Lawrence College and served as a moot court judge at Queen's University Law School. He was President of the Frontenac Law society for two years.

Lawrie McFarlane, PhD, served as Secretary of the Treasury Board, Deputy Minister of Advanced Education and Manpower, Deputy Minister of Education, and President and CEO of the Saskatoon Regional Health Board in Saskatchewan; Deputy Minister of Health, Treasury Board

Secretary, and Deputy Minister, Crown Corporations Secretariat, in British Columbia. He presently writes editorials for the *Victoria Times Colonist*. He is coauthor of *The Best Laid Plans: Health Care's Problems and Prospects*, and has written numerous policy editorials in the *Canadian Medical Association Journal*.

Index